There is a thin line that separates laughter and pain, comedy and tragedy, humor and hurt.

—Erma Bombeck

The colosseum erupted in an explosion of shouts, screaming, and applause as twenty-thousand people, packed wall-to-wall, jumped to their feet. Our organization's upline "Diamonds" strolled to the microphone with the confidence of royalty.

Her sequin-covered gown twinkled in the many lights shining from the ceiling. We could see from from our section in the cheap seats that her hands were covered in jewels when she adjusted the fur shawl around her shoulders.

"Ain't it great!" He screamed into the microphone. The crowd went nuts! "Ain't it great! Ain't it great!" chanted the brain-washed mob in perfect unison.

"Alright, alright, let's get started," he said with dynamic authority. A hush fell over the enormous crowd as they found their seats. All stadium lighting faded to black except for one spotlight illuminating the speaker.

The Diamond began his motivational talk — another in the long line of talks we'd heard that day. I fought drowsiness and fatigue while worrying about the boys between applause. My watch said 1:30am, and one more couple was slated to speak. Sleep deprivation. Were they doing it on purpose?

It was the *Summer of Dreams* business function, and one of the four yearly three-day conferences that all "serious" business-builders attended. If you didn't have the money, you were told to find it – beg, borrow or steal. Sell something, pick up cans, whatever you had to do to attend.

The sharp, motivated, business-building, paying-the-price distributors were required to attend. It was an unspoken but well-known rule. Missing any of the big-four functions was a sign that you weren't serious about your future. Absences were met with prompt sit-downs with upline – something you heard about and did everything in your power to avoid.

We were "core" team players who proved our love for business, family, and Jesus by attending every function... an idea promoted by those at the top.

Michael took notes in his worn Franklin planner with a rapid-fire shorthand. It wasn't real shorthand, just half sentences that only he could read.

I looked down our row to the left, to the right, then to the rear. Big smiles, winks of appreciation, and waves of acknowledgment poured my direction. I felt the tinge of warm fuzzies ooze down my back. A subtle smile of pride and accomplishment crept across my face.

Yes, we'd done it! Our first milestone in the business: Silver Direct Distributors. It was a rare accomplishment, but all were made to believe it was attainable.

And all those smiles, winks, and waves didn't come from strangers. They came from those under us: one hundred and forty-seven people representing ninety-seven distributorships were in the meeting with us.

"This many in a year," I thought to myself. It was August 1993. The previous twelve months had been rough. We'd endured verbal attacks and emotional rejection from family and friends for being in "the business".

People in our community laughed. "That thing's been through here; That thing doesn't work; I can't believe you'd be in a door-to-door thing; My brother-in-law did that thing back in the 70's and went broke; That business is saturated; You'll never make that thing work in this area; That thing won't work in rural places; You'll never make it!" they said.

We now sat in a stadium filled with twenty-thousand people from all over the country, with a hundred and forty-seven that were "ours." I could never have imagined being able to convince almost a hundred and fifty people to leave their kids for a weekend, spending money they didn't have, driving twelve hours through four states, all in the aim to build a business based on a dream; but it was Michael's ability. He built a dream in those people in a way I can't explain. It was an unbridled enthusiasm that he could take from himself and put into others. When Michael gets passionate about a thing – when he believes in something with his whole heart, nothing can stop him. I'd seen it so many times over the years. God had given him a dynamic personality and an ability to communicate ideas in ways I'd never seen before. He was determined to succeed. When someone told him a thing was impossible to achieve, his drive would rise a notch.

It'd been a year of phenomenal success and growth, but no money to show for our efforts. "Keep building it and the money will come," repeated our sponsors. "Just build it on faith."

During that year we had also purchased our first home. My brother had bought if after Grandma died and had lived in the home for several years. We purchased it from him for $36,000.00. There were three small bedrooms, one bath, and an unfinished basement. Every needed updating, but the boys would love growing up in the country as I did, and we were only a stone's throw from Mom and Dad's. It was, for all intents and purposes, a dream come true. I was home.

A few days after getting back from the three-day business conference, Eddie and Dana, our upline sponsors in the business, were coming by to see the house. It was a perfect opportunity to pull a prank they'd never forget. Dana would, we'd learned during the previous year, snoop through our bathroom cabinets in search of "negative" products (products purchased at a store rather than through the network marketing business). Everyone knew she did it, but she'd always deny it to their faces when asked.

"Let's fix her," said Michael about half and hour before they arrived.

"What are you going to do?" I asked.

"Grab a big piece of cardboard from one of your product boxes and meet me in the bathroom," he said through a mischievous tone.

We gathered in the bathroom a few minutes later; me with the cardboard and Michael with... marbles?

"Honey, take everything out of the medicine cabinet–,"

"What are you going to do?" I interrupted.

"We're going to fill this medicine cabinet with these," he replied with a smile. It was a bucket full of glass marbles.

"When they open the cabinet," he continued, "these will fall out all over the place! Trust me – it'll be hilarious!"

"But how are we going to—"

"I'll show you, just hurry," he interrupted.

The idea was simple: cover the opening of the cabinet with the cardboard as to make a temporary wall to hold the marbles in position. Pour in the marbles at the top edge, fill the space, then close the med-cabinet's mirrored door over the cardboard. Once the mirror is closed against the cardboard, slide the cardboard out from behind the mirror. The marbles stay inside the med-cab, loaded and ready to go.

We worked quickly together and prepared the prank.

"Dana is going to die when she opens that up!" I couldn't help but laugh at the thought. "But, do you really think she'll look inside?" I asked.

"Are you kidding?" responded Michael. "She can't resist the urge to find something negative in our house!"

An hour passed. We all sat together in our living room discussing the business.

"Jonetta, I've got to use the restroom. Is it okay?" Dana asked in her hyper-positive tone.

"Of course," I replied, matching her. I was about to bust. Eddie rambled on about new recruiting methods. I shot Michael a side-eye. He looked like the cat that ate the canary.

Dana screamed amid the crashing sound of marbles pouring from the cabinet, bouncing in and off the porcelain sink and floor. Eddie jumped to his feet and ran toward the bathroom.

"Dana," I yelled from the couch. "What are you doing in my medicine cabinet?" Tears rolled down our faces from laughter. Dana never, to my knowledge, snooped in our cabinets again.

Jonetta Shank

Chapter 8

The Price

Spring 1994

They who are of the opinion that money will do everything may very well be suspected to do everything for money.

—George Savile

The good times were few and far between. We'd became little more than business partners and roommates, but we presented ourselves as a "perfect couple" in public, because that's what success in the business required.

Truth be told, there was almost nothing left of our marriage. Michael lived to work and worked to live, having no room for anything else in his life. Our upline called it "paying the price."

"Pay the price that others won't pay to reach the life that others won't reach!" A phrase repeated in every motivational tape, book, and meeting.

Our upline "counseled" us on every aspect of life, and their suggestions were growing more bizarre by the week. Eddie told Michael to avoid media, newspapers, and television. Pay the price.

"Remove all the negative in your life – it'll slow your growth," said Eddie. Pay the price.

"Stay away from family and friends who are negative, or won't support your dreams," was a trending doctrine at the bigger meetings. Pay the price.

Our credit cards were maxed, but Eddie said, "Don't worry, the bonus checks will go up. Build the dream. You'll pay off everything when you hit Ruby!" Always another level. A bigger dream. Pay the price.

Michael was getting about four hours of sleep per night, and I didn't get much more. He had, for the past two years, done everything he was told to do to build the business: three motivational tapes a day, a book a week, showed the plan to seven new people a week, attended all the meetings, forced himself to be a hundred percent positive about everything, verbalized our goals daily, and didn't touch a negative product. Pay the price.

I operated my part of the business (i.e.; paperwork, product orders, attending meetings with him, managing the checkbook) all between trying to raise two small boys and running a household. Pay the price.

The accounting firm had announced that they were relocating their computer division from Carmi to Robinson, Illinois. They wanted us to relocate with them. Michael enjoyed the work immensely, but the low salary and microscopic commissions hadn't allowed us to pay the bills. It was an easy decision. We'd mortgaged a home and invested two years into our side business. Moving to Robinson wasn't in the cards.

Michael started looking for another job, but there were none to be had. Hundreds of out of work coal miners were, like Michael, looking for work, and the Good ol' Boy network was tough to crack.

The business was costing a fortune to maintain and grow. Gas, wear and tear on our vehicle, books, tapes, meals out, babysitters, function tickets, business travel, phone, tires, required every penny of any profits earned. Pay the price.

The business's books ran in the red, despite the profits. We were building the dream, but the dream had turned into a nightmare. We were paying the price, but at what cost? *For what shall it profit a man, if he shall gain the whole world, and lose his own soul?*

Filing bankruptcy was all that was left. Our finances, along with our marriage and spiritual lives, were bankrupt.

Our separation from family and friends, combined with the neglect of our faith, had changed the soil of our hearts. It became a soil where one thing could grow and thrive: sin.

The road to hell is paved with good intentions and reached through small steps.

There's a story of putting frogs in a cool pot of water sitting on a burner. The frogs pay no attention to the rising temperature because they enjoy the water. The water will boil, and they'll die in the pot, never jumping to save themselves because they don't feel the heat.

We slowly, in small steps, marched toward hell. We were frogs in a pot, held in place by our desire for financial success. We didn't feel the temperature rising. Paul told Timothy about the dangers accompanying desires of riches:

> *But those who desire to be rich fall into temptation and a snare, and into many foolish and harmful lusts which drown men in destruction and perdition. For the love of money is a root of all kinds of evil, for which some have strayed from the faith in their greediness, and pierced themselves through with many sorrows* (1 Tim. 6:9-10, NKJV).

What sorrows would pierce us? What snares would trap us? We had, during the past few years, wandered off our path toward a mirage of riches and false security offered by the "business". The business had been a lure that tempted us

Sister, hear and understand what I am about to say. Anything can be a lure. Anything. It could be friends, family, a job, hobby, social media – *anything* can be used as bait to lure you away from the path made by your Creator.

Solomon said:

Man's goings are of the Lord; how can a man then understand his own way? It is a snare to the man who devoureth that which is holy, and after vows to make enquiry. A wise king scattereth the wicked, and bringeth the wheel over them. The spirit of man is the candle of the Lord, searching all the inward parts of the belly. Mercy and truth preserve the king: and his throne is upholden by mercy. The glory of young men is their strength: and the beauty of old men is the grey head. The blueness of a wound cleanseth away evil: so do stripes the inward parts of the belly (Prov. 20:24-30).

Your adversary is a highly qualified being (Job 1:6) with a resume of experiences (Matt. 16:23) incorporated over thousands of years (1 Jo. 3:8). He has a plethora of skill-sets (2 Cor. 2:11) and talents in his arsenal (Gal. 6:11). He is incredibly difficult to recognize (Gen. 3:1), due to his ability to appear as beauty and light (2 Cor. 11:14). His words soothe itching ears (2 Tim. 4:3) and seduce our deepest desires (1 Tim. 4:1). He has a myriad of highly intelligent methods (2 Cor. 2:11) and complex strategies (Eph. 6:11) to cripple (2 Cor. 11:3) and conquer us (1 Pet. 5:8).

Recognize in your life what we were too young, too stupid, and too blind to see. Anything can become a lure to divert you from your true path. The "business" had become our lure.

Someone said, "One man's hindsight is another man's foresight." Sister, my hindsight can be your foresight. I hope you're paying attention, because wisdom is being placed into your hands.

Chapter 9

The Prayer

Late Summer 1994

Women marry men hoping they will change. Men marry women hoping they will not. So, each is inevitably disappointed.

—Albert Einstein

Michael found a job as a sales rep with a cellular phone company after the accounting firm removed their computer operations from Carmi, Illinois. The cell provider opened a new office in Harrisburg, and he became part of what they called, "The First Team." It was a commission-only sales job and that scared me to death, offered no salary or benefits, and the idea of supporting a family with a commission-only job was a scary thought, but certainly better than nothing.

Michael set company sales records his first month in, and the commissions totaled three times more than his monthly salary at his computer job. We were now, after several years, paying our bills. The relief was refreshing, but digging out from the depth of our financial hole was a challenge.

We continued to build our "side" business, but we couldn't hold the volume necessary to reach the Gold Direct Distributor level. Turn-over in our organization was high, as was the nature of network marketing.

The gospel of prosperity offered by the business had poisoned Michael's heart. My own life had veered so far from the Lord that I had no spiritual encouragement left to give. Any conviction I'd felt had vanished. I still hoped, at times, that we would eventually get back to God, but I'd stopped praying months before, feeling as though I was nothing more than a hypocrite. We'd closed our Bibles and disconnected from the church long ago. I wasn't about to cause God to be more disgusted with me than He already was by running back to Him with hat in hand. The thought seemed like mockery.

"Show up only when you need something," I could imagine Him saying. No, I wouldn't do that.

I could no longer do that one thing – it was the most precious, valuable, and powerful thing a woman could do for herself and family. I could no longer pray. And not for a lack of belief, but because of *pride*. No, I wouldn't be seen by God as a "user" – a rancid leech looking to Him only when it suited me.

Many who wore His name seemed concerned only when they were in need, as if He were their personal genie in a bottle to be rubbed in emergencies.

Our original hope to make a little extra side money in the business – money that was supposed to have been created from ten to fifteen spare hours a week, wasn't materializing. The extra $2,000.00 per month pitched to us by Eddie was real, but he had conveniently withheld information that would have prevented us ever getting involved: the costs associated with making the money. I was seeing that the business was a zero-sum game and knew that Michael would never be free from the monster we'd created.

If he continued working his full-time job and spending another thirty hours each week trying to build our side business, we'd have no chance of having a good marriage, and no chance of ever returning to the Lord.

Michael had changed a lot over the past few years, but I believed that *I* had *not* changed.

I still had faith, didn't I? Couldn't I just say a little prayer? Could I ask despite the abandonment of my faith?

I proceeded to do, with great reluctance, what I had been determined not to do… I prayed.

Dear Father in Heaven, please forgive me for my neglect, my lack of prayers to You. I pray for my husband and ask that you would do something that would wake him up to see how this pyramid business will finish us off if he doesn't stop. Show him how the cost of the things is just too much. Open his eyes, please. In Jesus name, Amen.

I rose from my prayer feeling pious.

Robert Barron once wrote, "We are exceptionally good at seeing the faults in others and exceptionally adept at ignoring the faults in ourselves." God was going to answer my prayers.

Girls, be careful what you ask for. You might just get it.

Chapter 10

The Pain

October 1, 1994

She's been through Hell and came out an angel. You didn't break her, darling. You don't own that kind of power.

—@bmmpoetry

Reliving life's most painful times aren't desirable nor easily done but must, for the sake of others, be revisited…

My world crashed down around me. A shock of cold blanketed my body surging upward, taking hold of my throat. A loud ringing flooded both ears as my heartrate doubled instantly. I dropped in place – no strength to stand. A bullet to the chest wouldn't have been as painful as this. It was an almost unbearable pain.

And the instantaneous emotional destruction? It may be best described as what is felt when receiving news of a death – the death of a loved one; the death of one that you love.

Finding that your spouse has been unfaithful is one of the most psychologically stressful events anyone can experience, and I cannot emphasize this enough.

It is a life-changing stress that can cause illness and depression, and it imposes a stress that you can't believe.

Stress (a state of mental or emotional strain or tension resulting from adverse or very demanding circumstances, Merriam-Webster, 2017)[1] affects our ability to manage during times and events we perceive to be out of our control and beyond our resources. The stress brought upon us by such an event can be catastrophic if not managed in the right way.

Stress is a psychological (and sometimes physical) weight, which begs questions like, "How much weight does a particular event apply? How much can I bear? What is too much? How do I cope? How do I get through this life event?

Finding out our spouse has been unfaithful is connected to almost all the top twelve stress events we experience in this life. This was revealed in Holmes and Rahe's Stress Scale[2], published over fifty-years ago, which measured forty-three life-events and their effects upon adults and children. Their research led them to assign stress weights, also called "Life Change Units" to each event. I've included the top-twelve life-events, along with their specific stress weights listed in the following table:

Adult Life Event	LCU	Child Life Event	LCU
Death of spouse	100	Death of parent	100
Divorce	73	Unplanned pregnancy/abortion	100
Marital separation	65	Getting married	95
Jail term	63	Divorce of parents	90
Death of close family member	63	Acquiring a visible deformity	80
Injury or illness	53	Fathering a child	70
Marriage	50	Jail sentence of parent (1+year)	70
Fired from job	47	Separation of parents	69
Marital reconciliation	45	Death of brother or sister	64
Retirement	45	Change in acceptance by peers	67
Change in health of family member	44	Unplanned pregnancy of sister	64
Pregnancy	40	Discovery of being an adopted child	63

The Holmes and Rahe results are important for several reasons that apply directly to you and your life. First, the psychiatrists chronicled and assessed the medical records of over five-thousand patients and found a direct correlation between the life event and illness (0.118 positive correlation). In other words, these events can and do cause sickness (the degree of physical, emotional and spiritual are unknown) in ourselves and our children.

Suffering marital infidelity is a type of death (100 and 63 on the chart, respectively) of your spouse. The one you've known and loved is no longer that person you've known and loved. It is a fundamental cause of separation (65) and divorce (73). It can potentially foster a *mental* (emotional) jail sentence (63) whereby we are tormented by the thoughts of the act. It can lead to self injury or physical sickness (53). The act of maintaining the marital relationship is stressful in itself (50), so maintaining the marriage after an affair is, at least, as stressful if not more. And what if the affair happened with your spouse's co-worker, leading to the demand that your spouse leaves that workplace (47)? If forgiveness is possible, the stress of reconciliation (45) still exists!

What about the negative affects on children? You and I can agree that the future of our children and those things that might be detrimental to them is of critical importance. Anything affecting our children becomes the *most* important thing(s) to consider.

For children, the death of a parent (100) is the greatest stress on a child's life. Divorce is closer to a parental death than any other life event. Separation (69) is the typical first-step, usually with divorce (90) following. This opens the door to another marriage (95). These weights are accumulative, and the long-term negative affects on our children is still, to a large part, unknown.

When you look at the stress weight of each life event, and how the stress of future decisions impact our kids, there's a lot to think about. Sister, this is the kind of knowledge that we need when these kinds of crisis land in our laps!

How well-adjusted are children who come from fatherless homes? An example might be found in a mass shooting that occurred at a high school in Parkland, Florida. Seventeen were killed and seventeen more wounded, making this one of of the world's deadliest school massacres. Mark Meckler, an American political activist and attorney, reported on February 27, 2018, that of the 27 deadliest mass shooters, 26 of them had one thing in common: they were fatherless[3].

Children need a two-parent home, as much as it is possible and in your control.

My world was destroyed when I'd found that Michael had cheated on me. The grizzly details of "how" I found out are irrelevant, but the chance of my boys growing up in a fatherless home were, at that point, very high.

How am I going to get through this? Is he really sorry? Does he want her? Why would he do such a thing to me, our children and our family? Does he want forgiveness? Can I possibly forgive him? If I can forgive him, can I live with this? Do I want to be with him beyond this point? If I forgive him, will we ever be happy again? Will we ever have trust in our relationship? Will I be able to believe anything he says? What will my family think? What will I do? Where will I go? What will my friends think? What will a divorce do to our children? Did I do something to cause this? Is she smarter or prettier or better in some way than I am? Do I want to try again with him? Should I divorce him and hope for someone else to come along? I feel like a fool! Am I a fool? How have other women gotten through this? Why would God let this happen to us — to me?

My mind raced. No appetite. No energy. Sorrow and grief consumed me. I wanted to go to him so badly, but hated him at the same time!

One moment I wanted to forgive and the next I wanted to tell him I hated him and for him to never come back.

My entire emotional balance was in shambles. The tears wouldn't stop and the pounding in my head grew worse. Time slowed to a halt. Death would be a relief to the unrelenting torture I now lived moment by moment.

I searched frantically for an answer. Anything to stop the pain. Everything seemed to point to divorce. Wouldn't divorce stop the pain? He was the source of the pain, so getting away from him meant getting away from the pain. And maybe God wanted me to divorce Michael. Jesus said in Matthew 5, *"But I say unto you, that whosoever shall put away his wife, saving for the cause of fornication, causeth her to commit adultery: and whosoever shall marry her that is divorced committeth adultery (v.19)."* He said it again in Matthew 19, *"And I say unto you, whosoever shall put away his wife, except it be for fornication, and shall marry another, committeth adultery: and whoso marrieth her which is put away doth commit adultery* (v.9)."

I could, according to my understanding of His words, divorce Michael. If I didn't remarry, so be it, but I *could* remarry because of his sexual sins.

Divorce would be fast, cheap, and easy – just like the tramp he'd been fooling around with. But was it the right solution for my and our boy's futures? How could I possibly know the answer to what would become of our future? God would show me what would become of us, wouldn't He?

Chapter 11

The Paradigm

[**par**-*uh*-dahym, -dim] **noun**:
1. an example serving as a model; pattern
2. cognitive framework containing the basic
assumptions, ways of thinking, and methodology that are
commonly accepted by members of a discipline or group[1]

A strong woman loves, forgives, walks away, lets go, tries again, and perseveres… no matter what life throws at her.

—unknown

A few days later and the pain hadn't subsided. My eyes were swollen from crying and my stomach ached from fasting – not a voluntary fast, just no appetite. The thought of food made me sick.

Michael was a wreck, as well. Good! I wanted him to suffer for what he'd done to us. He apologized incessantly and sincerely. We tried to talk but it was no use. I couldn't bear the sight of him.

I had to divorce him.

The world shouted, "Leave the no-good #@%*&!" The TV psychologist said, "Better to be from a broken home than to live in one." This was a glimpse into the cognitive framework shared by modern-day media. It was a paradigm also shared by family and friends.

I needed relief. Take my boys and run. Alimony? There wouldn't be any. Who cared. I needed what we all need – respite from discord and pain, restoration of peace, a feeling of security, emotional balance.

New love. A man who'd treat me like I deserved. A man with financial security. Maybe he would treat my boys like his own.

I was still young. I could attract another man. Maybe he'd sweep me off my feet, just as Michael had done years before.

A handsome, funny, nurturing-but-masculine, affectionate, communicative, spiritual, wise to the world, aggressive in business and sports, meek with children and puppies, giver to the poor and exalter of the underdog type of man.

A man who would make me a big bowl of popcorn and cry through the chic-flick I wanted to watch. A thoughtful, kind, generous, brave, considerate man who always put me and my boys before himself.

Yeah, I loved Michael. But I wasn't *in* love with him. I hadn't been *in* love with him for a long time, and he knew it. And, according to most everyone, that was reason enough. Add an affair into the mix and the decision was made to order.

My family was completely supportive of my decision. They cheered me on, becoming a rallying squad of encouragers, chanting in unison, "Leave him, leave him, leave him."

Those who raised me and loved me without condition wanted me to escape the chaos, and a quick divorce was, in their opinions, the best thing I could do for myself.

Oh, and don't forget my many friends who were thrilled to dispense unsolicited wisdom. They came out of the woodwork.

Friends. People who hadn't been in contact for years but were suddenly "there for me" with words of advice. The best advice seemed to pour from those who'd been divorced – some were on their second (even third) husbands. They advised me on the do's and don'ts of navigating a divorce like seasoned attorneys.

Yes, they all meant well as they parroted common catch-phrases: get out while you can, you've only got one life, enjoy your youth, kids are resilient, there's never been a better time to be single, get a tattoo, live a little, reinvent yourself, get a new career, family will help raise your kids, you'll be free to find your soulmate.

I became a veritable sound-board for the well-meaning women who'd lived through divorce and were now searching for *their* soulmates.

It was a watershed of attention from people who hadn't shown any concern for me in years. The new fame and attention bolstered my brokenness and lifted my confidence.

But was divorce the solution? If I flushed my problems and started over, would my boys and I be better off?

The thoughts of a new "soulmate" were seductive. A man so perfectly matched and in tune with me, my needs, my desires, my interests – a man with no baggage. The idea sent a tingle through my body. It sounded wonderful!

But the thoughts were interrupted by Dad's voice. "Jonetta, consider the source." My father was able to read people. He was pragmatic and realistic to a fault.

How credible were those offering advice? What fruit had they produced? How had their lives turned out so far?

And deeper still, where had these people been in my life? Were they willing to step in and help me with a mortgage payment, an electric bill, or groceries? Or how about at two in the morning when the baby was crying and covered in spit-up? Would they be there when I took a new job and needed help with the kids?

The admonishments to divorce Michael were seductive, and seemed to scratch the itch of vengeance deep within my soul.

But thank God that my parents raised me on a Bible foundation. As I considered the onslaught of advice, Proverbs 5 rushed into view:

> *For the lips of a strange woman drop as an honeycomb, and her mouth is smoother than oil: but her end is bitter as wormwood, sharp as a two-edged sword. Her feet go down to death; her steps take hold on hell* (vv.3-5).

I knew Solomon spoke here of sexual seduction, but luring words affect facets of life outside of the sexual domain. God's advice remained the same – be cautious and wise when being advised because what sounds good on the surface may lead to an end worse than the beginning.

Did my friends' advice come from a spiritual source? Could their words lead me and my children into deeper despair?

"Friends" often have nothing to lose. They have no skin in the game, so they won't bear any consequence from their advice.

Good discernment is critical and has a direct affect on outcome. It is about having the discipline to examine what you are told through the template of God's word.

Are our decisions during struggle defined by the Creator's advice? Do we seek out His advice over friends and family?

It's Job's story. His friends said and did some things that were right. They came to his aid, showed great empathy, and sacrificed their time for him – without giving advice or using him as a sounding board.

They were true friends who put their money where their mouths were.

But they blew it in that they couldn't keep their mouths shut. The three put a verbal diatribe on Job that included their opinions of God's disdain for Job because of his alleged sins.

But God said they offered man-made wisdom and didn't speak truth!

It didn't matter. I had to get out from under the stress of our life and away from the man I couldn't save.

"Lord, is this what you'd have me do? I know you work through people, so is this the answer? Leave him? You know I can't go on. It's too much. Please do something – please show me an answer!

"If you want me to divorce him or stay with him, I need you to show me – please show me—"

Knocking interrupted my prayers. I got up from the floor, wiped my eyes with a shirt sleeve and mustered a little strength to find out who it was.

"Suzie? What are you doing here?" I hadn't seen her in years.

"Jonetta," she said reaching to me with a hug. "I heard. I'm so sorry," she whispered into my ear. Tears flowed again.

"Come in, come in," I said, pulling her into our small house. Michael was at work and the boys were playing at Nana's. "Can I get you something to drink?"

"Tea if you've got it," Suzie said with a smile. She dropped into a recliner and let her purse fall to the floor next to her.

"God, you look awful!" she blurted as I handed her the drink.

"Thanks a lot — just what I needed to hear," I said flatly.

"No, no, I'm sorry — I didn't mean it like—"

"I know you didn't," my words interrupted her apology.

"Jonetta, I don't have much time, but I needed to talk to you." Suzie leaned back and sipped the tea. She looked old and haggard, and it shocked me. We hadn't seen each other since graduation.

"Sure, Suzie. What is it?"

"You know I've never been religious," she began, "but I've always believed in God."

"Yeah, I know that," I replied with as much encouragement as I could generate.

"My husband cheated on me, too!" Suzie almost screamed. I jumped from the couch and ran to her. We wept together for a good ten minutes or so.

Suzie wasn't there to support me in my time of grief. She needed someone to share the loss with her. Someone who truly understood what she was going through.

I would, over the next three hours, find out a lot about Suzie's life since graduation. She had, like me, married her high-school sweetheart. And she, like me, had two children with him. But that's where the similarity of our past lives ended. Her first husband had an affair and she divorced him, taking her two young girls with her. She remarried and had a child with her second husband. Then, with three kids under the age of six years old, she had an affair with her second husband's best friend! This wasn't the girl I'd grown up with.

Suzie gave every gory detail. I cried throughout the conversation, feeling every moment of anger, pain, and suffering. And those poor kids.

Her second husband forgave her affair with his best friend and begged her to stay, but she was "in love" with the best friend. So, she filed a petition for divorce from husband number two and moved in with his best friend – a man who became husband number three. She married him one day following the order of dissolution from husband number two.

And the man who had cheated on her? Husband number three. *If they'll do it with you, they'll do it to you!* Do I need to repeat that?

Suzie slumped on my living room floor surrounded by piles of wadded tissues. She was twenty-seven, and her life was a disaster. Three children with two different men and man number three has found a new lover.

"I've got an idea!" Suzie said with a new and strange excitement.

"What?" I asked.

"We can find a house to rent… together!" Her face seemed to glow and contort at the suggestion.

And there it was. God's answer to my prayers came in those next few seconds. A new life flashed through my mind. Suzie and I in a rent-house with five young kids. New careers, her wanting to go clubbing every other night, and me raising my boys in that environment.

"Suzie, I appreciate you coming by," I said as I picked up nasty tissues strewn over the floor. She got up quickly and grabbed her purse.

"Here's my number — call me tonight, okay? We can start house-hunting tomorrow!"

"Thanks, Suzie. Yeah, let's just see what happens," I coaxed her toward the door. She left with a big smile and a dance in her step. She paused outside the door, spun around with a smile and exclaimed, "We could get matching tattoos!"

I laughed and closed the door. *Matching tattoos?*

No, Suzie wasn't the person I'd known years before. Her life was broken, and her kids were a mess.

Thinking about the condition of her children's lives brought me to a stark realization of what could become of my own children's lives.

I can divorce Michael, but my boys cannot. He will always be a part of their lives, and rightfully so — he's their father. If we go down the this path, whether it be me or him or both, it will become a legacy to those boys. Right or wrong, this decision will impact our kid's lives today. It will impact them for all eternity.

I broke down again.

"Thank you, Father. Thank you, thank you!" I had begged God to show me. To give me direction, and He had done the very thing I'd asked! The answer came through Suzie, and the visualization of what life could become in short order. Yes, God works through people.

I rose from my prayers toward a specific resolve: divorce was not, at least for me and at that time, the answer. I would try to forgive Michael, but a huge fear remained. Could I live with the fact that he'd had an affair? Could I forgive this man? Could I remain in this small town, among the rumors, gossip, and shame?

I threw Suzie's phone number in the trash can, then dialed his office.

Michael's secretary answered and patched me through to his desk.

"Come home," I said softly. "We need to talk."

Chapter 12

The Phoenix

[fee-niks] **noun**:
1. a mythical bird of great beauty fabled to
live 500 or 600 years in the Arabian wilderness, to burn itself on a
funeral pyre, and to rise from its ashes in the freshness of youth and
live through another cycle of years: often an emblem of immortality
or of reborn of idealism or hope.
2. genitive **Phoenicis** [fee-**nahy**-sis,, -**nee**-] (*initial capital letter*)
Astronomy. a southern constellation between Hydrus and Sculptor.
3. a person or thing of peerless beauty or excellence; paragon.
4. a person or thing that has renewed or restored after suffering
calamity or apparent annihilation.[1]

There is no force equal to a woman determined to rise.

—W.E.B. Dubois

Stay with Michael? Keep our family in tact? Could I forgive him? Could I really live with this? Was forgiveness possible? Would our life ever be the same? Could it be better? Was staying with him the best decision for me? Was it best for my future?

The answers are clear when you look at our life today: we'll celebrate our thirty-third wedding anniversary this year (2018). I've never been happier! The depth of our love for one another is at a level that can't possibly be described in words. I have a feeling of security and satisfaction that is beyond description, with a great excitement for our future! Woman, our life today is truly amazing – better than I could have ever imagined! We have four amazing sons who are socially proficient, well-adjusted young men, each with an outstanding work ethic. They are givers of themselves, ambitious young men of fine character. Michael always wants to give me the credit for raising them, but they wouldn't be who they've become without his part in raising them.

We also enjoy the blessings of a family business that seeks to serve God in all that we do, a home filled with laughter, peace, contentment, love, security, and a happiness that would have never been realized had I chosen a different path.

Michael has become *the* man that I always wanted and the man I knew he could become.

Please know that none of this is written to brag or boast. I share it with you in a sincere desire to show you what forgiveness can bring to your future.

It is also vitally important that you understand I make no judgment of any kind toward any woman for the decisions she has made in her life. No person, in my opinion, can stand in judgment of another for decisions made within times of abuse, neglect, or hopelessness. And I have, needless to say, neither wisdom nor desire for comparative judgments upon others, especially for those who have suffered experiences that I know little to nothing about.

Judging a woman for her past decisions is, in my opinion, nothing more than pietistic female egotism.

Sister, know this: if I can do it, you can do it. The depth of love and happiness that can be created in your marriage, regardless of the past, is beyond your wildest imagination.

Your future *can* bring you levels of happiness and security that may seem impossible at this point in your life. This is faith… the substance of things hoped for and the evidence of things not seen. Without faith it's impossible to please God, for he who comes to God must believe that He is, and that He is a rewarder of those who diligently seek Him (Heb. 11:6).

The intimidating concept of faith is the conscious, willful act of putting belief into what looks impossible, based on something you can't even see, all of which rides on nothing more than hope. Yeah, it sounds nuts.

In other words, here's some invisible evidence, and I want you to believe in something not possible because of this invisible thing – both of which you must hope are true and possible, so that you can have what's impossible.

Sister, that's hope against hope.

It took three days of talks for me and Michael to reach a point where we could communicate. It had been three days of sheer hell.

Three days of crying, anguish, confusion, anger, and yelling through tears. Three days on a roller-coaster of emotional outbursts, cursing, fatigue and absolute brokenness. Three days of trying to manage life with work, meals, children, laundry and long to-do lists.

But inside that horrible thing called adultery I found a wonderful hidden treasure – it re-opened our lines of communication. We had previously fallen into a routine of work, business, kids, bills, and our communication had been neglected to the point that we were no longer able to share our deepest thoughts and emotions. We had "fallen" into marital stagnation. A state whereby two organisms conjoined into one flesh had been beaten into a numbness by the cruel hands of routine, familiarity, and boredom.

A second benefit I recognized, but initially resented with hatred and anger, was how the event forced me to look within myself, forcing me to examine my own flaws and deficiencies. Woman, this is the key to you.

I enjoy listening to Dr. Jordan Peterson, the clinical psychologist and professor at the University of Toronto, because his philosophy speaks to so many "common sense" principles in the human condition. He once said, "To change the world you must first change your world, and that begins with you – your competence, your talents…" Sister, change begins with you.

He said, "If your world is in chaos, pull back, look inward, and fix *yourself.* Then, and only then, can you hope to begin to fix your world!"

I wanted to fix my world but doing so required me to first look within… to look at what I needed to fix.

Through my willingness to forgive Michael for his sin of adultery, I could see that things certainly *could* be better than they were at that moment. However, it had to begin with me if I had any hope for a different and better future. The idea framed the question: what did I need to do with myself to make a better future a reality?

I knew that divorce wasn't the best solution for me or our children for a host of reasons. Divorce, as best I could tell seeing it happen in the lives of others, looked like a train wreck. It was devastating and produced a no-win situation almost every time.

But not divorcing meant that I had to reestablish trust. Michael had destroyed my trust by his unfaithfulness. Trust would be – no, it "had" to be earned over time, but offering trust leads to a quandary many find difficult to overcome: how do you trust when trust is broken? If trust is earned over time, immediate trust is impossible to achieve; yet, trust is the necessary component for *any* attempt at reconciliation.

The answer is to understand that any extension of trust you generously gift to the perpetrator of adultery is not based on feelings of trust. In other words, you don't trust him in your heart, right? But you don't make the choice to give trust based on the existing feelings because your feelings say that there is not trust. You give trust voluntarily, by choice – based on the idea of faith over the opposing feelings of your heart.

Your decision says, "I will give you my immediate trust, even though I don't feel trust for you and because you do not deserve my trust."

If you can do this, and if he does everything in his power, that trust will come back to your heart and your relationship. It will be stronger than before, but it takes a long time.

And sister, this presupposes certain criteria: is he truly ashamed, repentant, and sorrowful from his heart? Has he ended the affair and taken the steps to demonstrate that he wants you and only you? Will he shut up and listen to you rant, scream, and assault him with your tongue over what he has done to you, your children, and your future? Is he now trying his very best to prove that he wants, more than anything else, to make things right with your marriage relationship?

If your man is doing these things, you have a foundation whereby you can give him your trust and forgiveness.

I can forgive but I can't forget! You are right, and this might be the very reason why Jesus provided what people call the "exceptive clause" in His statements.

Matthew 13:3-9 says:

The Pharisees also came unto him, tempting him, and saying unto him, Is it lawful for a man to put away his wife for every cause? And he answered and said unto them, Have ye not read, that he which made them at the beginning made them male and female, and said, For this cause shall a man leave father and mother, and shall cleave to his wife: and they twain shall be one flesh? Wherefore they are no more twain, but one flesh. What therefore God hath joined together, let not man put asunder. They say unto him, Why did Moses then command to give a writing of divorcement, and to put her away? He saith unto them, Moses because of the hardness of your hearts suffered you to put away your wives: but from the beginning it was not so. And I say unto you, Whosoever shall put away his wife, except it be for fornication, and shall marry another, committeth adultery: and whoso marrieth her which is put away doth commit adultery.

Jesus said the two will become one flesh joined together by God, and that no man should separate.

The Pharisees questioned Him again over their divorce laws and Jesus clarified His point. Whoever divorces except for the reason of adultery and remarries commits adultery.

I bring this text to light in an effort to reveal my understanding of His words and to highlight a simple possibility within His reasoning (I'm not going to debate the details or variety of interpretations, so kindly discard any ideas of emailing me to engage in a "nice" Bible argument). Jesus seemed to offer one justifiable reason for divorce and remarriage: adultery.

But if God joins two flesh into one, why mention *any* exceptive clause? Is it possible that God knows of man's inability to forget the past? Jeremiah wrote in 31:34, "*…for I will forgive their iniquity, and I will remember their sin no more.*" God not only has the ability to forgive, He can selectively forget – a talent no man or woman has. Man's lack of any ability to truly "forget" a thing might cause his inability to live with a thing.

There was an additional burden to be dealt with – my extended family. I could try to forgive Michael, but could they? Sharing too much about your marriage with family (relatives outside of your home) is a bad idea. When you seek their support during difficult times by telling them every detail, they become "fixed in time" by that event. Your problems at home may be repaired over time, but their attitudes (perceptions and feelings created in them when you revealed infractions by your spouse) are just as they were when you spoke with them.

You and your mate are moving forward in your mended relationship, but the damage done by them knowing may never be repaired. Wisdom says, "Keep private matters private".

Regardless of the damage that either of us had done, I had to try to forgive and forget. I had to rise from the ashes of life. The alternative was to give up. I wasn't willing to do that… yet.

Chapter 13

The Potential

I, with a deeper instinct, choose a man who compels my strength, who makes enormous demands on me, who does not doubt my courage or my toughness, who does not believe me naïve or innocent, who has the courage to treat me like a woman.

—Anaïs Nin

Strong, independent, intelligent women want a concrete reason to exercise faith when our faith and trust has been annihilated. We're not interested in "group" think or collectivism; we seek individuality. We want to stand on our own two feet. We want to be respected for our ideas and opinions, not placated or ignored. We find the ploy of "victimhood" repulsive.

We still need a good reason to trust again – to feel confident that if we again trust our man, he won't carelessly throw it away and break our heart – again! Or something like that, right?

What is one good reason? Forget the evident ones like: invested time, energy, emotions, feelings, your dwelling, good times, children, pets, material belongings, etc.

The one good reason is potential. Sounds canned or childish?

Ira and Ann Yates lived in a small, remote, west Texas community at the southeastern part of Pecos

County. It was a remote land of endless nothingness as far as the eye could see. Pioneers called it hardscrabble.

Mr. and Mrs. Yates had purchased a ranch and now, in 1925, were struggling to put food on the table and clothes on their backs. The bank pressed for late mortgage payments. Back taxes mounted. The wolves of failure and destitution stalked the Yates.

Out of options and losing all hope, Ira gave permission for oil exploration to Transcontinental Oil Company. In late October of 1926, when Ira and Ann stood at the precipice of financial ruin, Transcontinental hit oil.

It was found only a thousand feet below their barn and would later become one of the largest oil finds in American history, having produced over a billion barrels of oil by 1998.

Untapped potential.

You could have a million dollars in your checking account, but you'd never write a check on it if you didn't know it was there.

And that is the condition of many today. Today's woman has an abundance of riches she knows little about, and the great challenge is getting her to believe it's there.

You have unlimited spiritual riches supplied by God through Christ (Eph. 1:3) at your disposal. Tapping into His resources require trust and faith when looking across the hardscrabble landscape of your current situation.

Sister, to begin at this place is the hardest step. Visualizing potential (your man's potential, your relationship's potential, the potential for greater love, trust, intimacy, and communication) is faith.

Potential is part of the veritable substance (that of which a thing consists; physical matter or material) of things hoped for; it is the *evidence* of things *not seen*.

If you're at life's crossroads facing insurmountable odds and wanting only to escape, it is potential that births a new faith in the future. This new faith makes the bed for trust, and trust is the gateway to those hopes: communication, love, security, intimacy, affection, harmony, and happiness.

Faith represents action toward what can't be seen, generating inertia in the direction of our hopes, making manifest His instruction, "Walk by faith, not by sight (2 Cor. 5:7)."

Seeing the potential brings you to phase two: build the derrick.

Chapter 14

The Platform

Most women want a man that's already established; a strong woman will be part of his struggle, survive it, succeed together and build an empire.

—unknown

You've got to have a drilling derrick if you're ever going to reach the riches of potential. It sounds weird but it's a metaphor, so go with it.

How do we, as women, build the derrick so that we can get to the potential in our man and our relationship?

Prep the site:

Acknowledge what's in your way. Michael has said many times, "Women's lives are more complex than men's." This complexity is, in most cases, better managed by women, which may be why we remember that we were not created to do what men can do. We were created to do what men *can't* do. Women were created to do what men cannot do.

Women can become consumed by life's mundane repetition: child care, food, shopping, financial management, home care, taxi services, cleanliness in all things, human resources, task management, laundry services, health and well-being for everyone, menus, appointments, a business, ad nauseum. The sheer volume and complexity is overwhelming.

Our daily responsibilities are obstacles that can prevent us from building the derrick. And, strictly speaking, it's tough to build the derrick when we're so busy doing the immediate.

You've got to carve out (steal away) some time from the pressing things. Some call it "taking time for myself". Whatever you must do to find the time will be worth it.

In that time for yourself, think on and pray about the potential of your marital relationship. What does your potential marriage look like?

Meditate on their strengths and talents instead of dwelling on their flaws and mistakes. Focus on three things you love most about them.

Assemble the derrick: self examination. Looking inward instead of outward gives you and I the chance to see and remove the obstacles that have kept us from the rich reserves of potential.

It's a tough business, and unnatural to our first instinct. Our knee-jerk reaction is to look outward.

Why did God let this happen to me? Why did my husband do what he did? I'm a victim. It's someone else's fault. I'm good — others are evil. I'm right — you're wrong. Look at what others have done...

Laying blame on everything and everyone else is the easiest thing to do. It's not only the laziest thing to do, it's also the most damaging thing you can do to yourself, your family, and your future.

Yes, looking inside is extraordinarily difficult, and hideous to the extreme. Sometimes women dishonestly examine themselves.

I'm a great person. I have no sins. My faults are few. I don't need to change anything. If they can't accept me for who I am, they know where they can go! You know where this thinking leads. Look at the world around you.

Confronting your true self risks seeing your own flaws, your sins, and your ineptness. The image might be an ugly picture.

Self-examination is a concept rejected by today's culture and has led to many extremist positions becoming commonplace in society. For example, four-year-old boys who claim identity as "girls" are used by specific groups, along with the media, to win the acceptance and tolerance agenda battle.

Now, I make no claims whether these children do or do not feel as though they might be, in their hearts, different than their biological anatomy. I am, however, concerned and disturbed that adults promote such things for a population who have no life experience, no knowledge, nor wisdom, and no ability to measure the consequences of their actions. They are only kids.

Forgive me for the digression, but intelligent women need to be brutally honest when examining themselves. We need to recognize the dangerous post modernistic philosophy of Acceptance Without Regard. The idea is pushed ardently by Hollywood and media, and states that all progressive thought relating to the feelings and desires of those who choose to live their personal beliefs and behaviors which oppose patriarchal normatives (e.g., male leadership, women staying at home to raise children, etc.) must be 1) accepted by, and 2) free from any and all criticism(s) by others, as 3) criticisms originate only in racists, bigots, the uneducated, misogynists, etc.

In other words, if a middle-aged man declares that he "identifies" as a five-year-old girl, society must:

1) Accept that he is a five-year-old girl

2) Refrain from all criticism against his claim, including access to things specifically designated for young females (e.g. female restrooms)

3) Those who oppose are automatically labeled (in some cases they are attacked)

Why is it important to recognize the danger of this philosophy? It prevents honest self-examination. If a man suddenly "identifies" as a young female, should he not consider his own mind and heart? Wouldn't he be led to question his feelings and emotions? "Am I a middle-aged man, or a five-year-old girl? Why am I having these thoughts? Is it possible that I have a mental healthcare issue that needs evaluated by professionals? Will assuming that I am a five-year-old girl have an impact on my existing relationships, my career, or my well being?"

Those who throw their hands in the air and exclaim, "Okay, you're a five-year-old girl" do the man a severe injustice by robbing him of his own responsibilities of self-examination and reason; yet, they will accuse those who protest of being intolerant and narrow minded.

The illustration points to a salient fact that affects each one of us at the most fundamental level: we must fix ourselves before trying to fix others.

Is there a log in your eye? Is something crippling your vision (jealousy, bitterness, resentfulness, hatred, selfishness, unhealthy desires)?

"What do I need to fix in myself?" Brutal honesty reveals the issues as does your conscience, in most cases.

Paul said, "Examine yourselves, whether ye be in the faith; prove your own selves. Know ye not your own selves, how that Jesus Christ is in you, except ye be reprobates (2 Cor. 13:5)?"

It's a painful part of the process, like trying to clean a wound on our child… they kick and cry and scream. It's not much different when trying to clean up our own wounds. If we choose not to clean our wound, infection follows. What will infection do to your life?

Secure the work: ensure that the components are able to withstand the pressures that will be put upon it requires fastening and securing it all together.

You secure your derrick with vision – the desire to imagine and strive toward a great but unseen life. Solomon wrote, "Where there is no vision, the people perish (Prov. 29:18)." Why did you fall in love with your man? What did you see in him? What did you want your life to look like?

If you can reach the potential that is possible in your marriage, what will it look like? Remember these things and think seriously about what could be. Paul said, "Whatsoever things are true, whatsoever things are honest, whatsoever things are just, whatsoever things are pure, whatsoever things are lovely, whatsoever things are of good report; if there be any virtue, and if there be any praise, think on these things (Phi. 4:8)."

Get final approval: never start with an inspection. You shouldn't drill without an inspection and approval, but who has the authority?

God.

The principles of prayer and examination are prominently scattered throughout scripture, and an often-overlooked truth is found in 1 Peter 3:7:

Likewise, ye husbands, dwell with them according to knowledge, giving honor unto the wife, as unto the weaker vessel, and as being heirs together of the grace of life; that your prayers be not hindered.

We realize that Paul was speaking to husbands, but the reality that our prayers can be hindered applies to mankind, whether husband or wife. For God to hear and answer our prayers, we must live with our spouse in a way that communicates respect and bestows honor.

This premise affects our relationship with God to an extent surpassing even that of our spouse. Jesus asked of the Father to forgive us of our sins as we forgive those who have sinned against us. Peter magnified this in an extrapolation of Christ's teaching, "Not rendering evil for evil, or railing for railing: but contrariwise blessing; knowing that ye are thereunto called, that ye should inherit a blessing. For he that will love life, and see good days, let him refrain his tongue from evil, and his lips that they speak no guile: Let him eschew evil, and do good; let him seek peace, and ensue it. For the eyes of the Lord are over the righteous, and his ears are open unto their prayers: but the face of the Lord is against them that do evil."

Yes, it is biting when we realize that our resentment, anger, and vengeance must be released, contingent upon our own decision of offering sublime grace unto those who are the source of our pain and wrath. It is in this tortuous act that we are forgiven by God of our sins.

What else hinders your prayers? Peter also wrote, "But the end of all things is at hand: be ye therefore sober, and watch unto prayer (1 Pet. 4:7)." In modern words, be alert and of sober mind.

Do you want God to be active in your life? Have you grown weary of feeling that God is surreal or distant? Do you want to sense His presence with a renewed confidence that He is working all things together for the good – for *your* good?

Examine yourself. Realize once again that your connection with God is completely dependent upon your alertness of the adversary's pursuit of your weaknesses, your decision to live soberly, your attitude of respect to your spouse and others, and your willingness to forgive every transgression made against you from every person in your life, both past and present.

Make yourself right with God. Jesus said, "If you love me, keep my commandments (Jo. 14:15)." Do these things and God will place you within a unique, powerful place occupied by those He hears:

> *The righteous cry, and the Lord heareth, and delivereth them out of all their troubles. The Lord is nigh unto them that are of a broken heart; and saveth such as be of a contrite spirit. Many are the afflictions of the righteous: but the Lord delivereth him out of them all* (Psa. 34:17-19).

Prepare your drilling site by accepting that you were put here to do what men cannot do. Carve out time to meditate and pray. Meditate on your partner's strengths and potential. Focus on at least three things that you love about them.

Piece together your drilling derrick with an honest, thorough examination of your self. Confront your true self so that you can see the log in your eye. Fix the things only you can fix. Decide to be better today than you were yesterday. Fight through the tenderness and discomfort you feel when cleaning your wounds. Quit worrying about fixing others first – you can't fix anyone until you fix yourself.

Fasten it all together with the kind of vision your Father will be pleased with. Adopt an outlook of things which can be true, honest, just, pure, lovely, virtuous, and of good report.

You wanted to know how I got through life's most devastating events, enjoying a better life than I ever thought possible? I am giving you the secrets.

Chapter 15

The Pressure

Prayer is not an old woman's idle amusement. Properly understood and applied, it is the most potent instrument of action.

—Mahatma Gandhi

Your derrick is finished. You're ready to drill. What are you drilling for? The riches of "what can be".

Drilling requires force. Force produces friction. Friction produces heat. Heat causes fire. Fire destroys all, so learn how to manage force and friction. If you forget all of this, don't forget the next part:

The derrick was necessary for the drill; the drill is necessary to reach the potential you envision. The drill is the machine, but a bit is required. Your drill has a diamond-covered bit able to cut through life's barren surface – ground littered with tragedy and suffering, often without any sign of the treasure below.

What is your diamond-covered bit? Prayer.

Prayer is the one and only tool capable of reaching that endless pool of potential that is within every relationship, regardless of condition. Prayer is the least and most anyone can do. Prayer is the great power connecting us to God through His Son, and it is the great lever of action offered to those in Jesus Christ.

But beware. There's an element that will break your bit every time it is encountered: the almost impenetrable rock of pride.

Pride will not only destroy your bit, it will destroy everything you've worked so hard to achieve. Solomon said, "Pride goes before destruction (Prov. 16:18)." Pride creates two metaphorical by-products when drilling: friction and heat. Selfish pride gives way to marital friction. Friction heats spousal tempers that can start a firestorm in your marriage; therefore, start with pride, its potential, and how to overcome.

I have, over three decades, discussed marriage and divorce, as well as a variety of ancillary topics, with dozens of people. The experiences ranged from entertaining to bizarre and inspiring to heart-breaking. And, looking back, there seems to be a clear common denominator found within the majority of those divorces. That denominator is demonstrable in appearance. Selfish pride.

"*Too little, too late; he stopped fulfilling me; I was no longer in love; I was done; wasn't putting up with any more; I was better than that; I deserved better; I outgrew him; I found something new; found someone new; I couldn't forgive him for* (insert infraction)."

I'm not judging but am only sharing the common verbiage put forth as the "straw that broke the camel's back," so to speak. Unsolicited references to personal faults seemed rare, at best, which maybe why many attitudes seemed to put the onus on the ex-spouse.

At any rate, it makes me wonder about those "old school" wedding vows Michael and I said to each other – vows I took seriously.

I'll try to remember my vows without digging out our thirty-plus year-old VCR tape. They went something like, "I, Jonetta, take you, Michael, to be my lawfully wedded husband, to have and to hold, from this day forward, for better, for worse, for richer, for poorer, in sickness and in health, until death do us part."

Better, worse, richer, poorer, sickness, health, until death separates us. Did I mean the things I said? Things I vowed in the presence of many friends, family, and God? Sure, the best reason in the world for a divorce was in my hands. It was the only exception the Lord seemed to offer to obtain a justifiable divorce, right?

This was the first step in my own self examination and gave me a lousy feeling. It brought my integrity into question and caused me to wonder about the depth of my commitments.

Pride comes from the Adversary. It fosters inappropriate self-exaltation. Pride renders the holder powerless to look inward as it, simultaneously, impedes the ability to forgive.

Pride ensures no room for God, for God said, "The wicked, through the pride of his countenance, will not seek after God: God is not in all his thoughts (Psa. 10:4)."

Isaiah said, "For the day of the Lord of hosts shall be upon every one that is proud and lofty, and upon every one that is lifted up; and he shall be brought low (Isa. 2:12)."

Isaiah talked about God's plan for those who allow pride to rule their lives, as he wrote in 23:9, "The Lord of hosts has purposed it, to bring to dishonor the pride of all glory, to bring into contempt all the honorable of the earth."

Pride absolutely destroys and destroys absolutely.

"But he was unfaithful!" I said to myself over and over. *"I'm not putting up with this!"* My emotions raged. *"He's got to pay."* Pride battled forgiveness and humility. *"Jesus said when we lust in our hearts, we've committed adultery – so I'm just as guilty,"* I admitted. *"IF you can't forgive, you can't be forgiven,"* said the Bible.

"*Love keeps no record of wrongs. It trusts and hopes and perseveres,*" scriptures fought back.

"*Does it really say that or is it my bad memory?*" I went to my Bible. Philippians 4:8 says:

> *Finally, brethren, whatsoever things are true, whatsoever things are honest, whatsoever things are just, whatsoever things are pure, whatsoever things are lovely, whatsoever things are of good report; if there be any virtue, and if there be any praise, think on these things.*

If you and I can apply these things that Paul wrote about a very real and practical type of love, it will force us to become the very thing that prevents friction and reduces heat. Humility.

Drilling, oil rigs, derricks – it's a man's metaphor, no doubt! But I don't know a better way to describe the potential of the riches you possess just below that hidden surface of your relationship... or the potential waiting to be found in your horse.

The landscape, as you know, of your marriage may be beautiful or it may be desolate; but in either case there is a vast ocean of potential waiting under your feet. Friend, if you apply the industrial lubrication of humility to the diamond drill-bit of prayer, having properly constructed the derrick beforehand, nothing will prevent you from reaching a life that is so much better than what you might be living at this moment.

Flood the bit with humility (Eph. 4:2) being clothed in humility (Col. 3:12), and He will lift you up (Jas. 4:10) and give you favor (Jas. 4:6).

And sister, humility doesn't turn you into a doormat – it enables *Him* to bring *you* to those things you hope most for. It's His good pleasure to give it to you. "Even by the God of thy father, who shall help thee; and by the Almighty, who shall bless thee with blessings of heaven above, blessings of the deep that lieth under, blessings of the breasts, and of the womb (Gen. 49:25)."

Chapter 16

The Parching

October 1994

I believe in being strong when everything seems to be going wrong.

—Audrey Hepburn

Traffic on 145 from Paducah toward Harrisburg had been light for a Friday night. The boys, now 4 and 2, slept soundly in their respective car-seats behind us. Country music played at a low volume. Michael and I rode silently, both lost in thought.

"You okay," he asked. The question startled me.

"Yeah, fine." I replied.

"The mall was busy," said Michael.

"Halloween shoppers," I replied. Kentucky Oaks Mall was a popular weekend destination in and around Paducah. Tonight's crowd had been unusually thick. My eyes were telling me to get to bed. I checked the dashboard – 11:45pm. The hum of the tires didn't help matters. *Just twenty minutes and we'll be home.*

It had been a few weeks since "finding out," and Michael was doing everything in his power to make it up to me. Our communication had been as good as it had been since we'd left Nashville. I was gaining a grip on my emotional mountains and valleys, putting effort into love and forgiveness. I vacillated between an appreciation for our re-made relationship and wanting to kill the idiot!

But, as strange as it may sound, his unfaithfulness broke us out of bad habits and mind-numbing routines. It made us evaluate what was important to the both of us and gave us a glimpse into what we both had to lose.

Michael was ashamed of himself, but it was more than that. The guilt of his actions seemed to chain him. Yes, I forgave him, but he wasn't forgiving himself.

I'd overheard him a few nights before. He was in the bathroom… praying. It's embarrassing to admit, but I huddled against the closed door trying to hear his words. Now I wish I hadn't. It was a childish thing to do, but even worse was hearing someone's most private petitions to God.

Have you ever listened to someone's private prayers? Admissions of a hatred for self? Confessions of self hate amid pleas for Divine forgiveness? Weeping over one's own sin – when the one weeping has no idea anyone can hear, it is bone-chilling.

And part of me rejoiced. *Let him hurt like I hurt – he hurt me so bad! He made his own bed* (pardon that unintended pun). Yeah, I know. Awful, right?

"Michael," I sat up. "Something's burning." *Is the car on fire?*

"Yeah, honey. I smell it," he replied with concern in his words. "The gauges look fine. We're a mile from the house. It's probably nothing."

"Smells like trash – somebody's burn barrel is still going," I said.

We topped the hill and Michael locked down the brakes! Many large red trucks, emergency lights, people in the road. *God help them—*

Then I saw a flame shoot upward over dark tree-tops, lighting the sky. *Our house! No, God! No, no, no – this can't be happening!*

Michael held firm on the brakes. I don't know how the car didn't skid. He popped the door handle while slamming the car into park. His door flung open.

"Michael!" I screamed while managing to open my door. He was running toward the house. Flames flashed, illuminating black smoke bellowing from the roof. I unfastened my boys, both screaming with fear, and carried both to the edge of the front yard.

Mom rushed to me. I handed her the kids and turned to find Michael. A fireman in full uniform had him on the ground. Others were helping hold him in place. I dropped where I stood, onto freshly made mud and soot.

It's just a bad dream. Wake up.

"Jonetta," my dad's voice jolted me back to reality. I could feel his strong hands around my shoulders. "Get up, honey. It's gonna be okay," he said in the kindest voice. I clawed at his torso trying to stand. His eyes – the bluest I'd ever seen, looked into mine. We hugged tightly, crying quietly within deafening sirens, emergency lights, and a smoke that I pray never to smell again.

I sat in mom's antique rocker watching our boys sleep. We'd bathed, changed, and played for a while hoping to sooth their minds. They were finally asleep.

Michael was still up at the house dealing with the aftermath. I could hear the trucks pull away. Mom's clock chimed. 4:00am.

How much more could I take? Lord, what is it? What have I done?

He won't put more on me than I can bear. No. That's not what it says – not what it means. It says that he won't allow me to be tempted beyond my ability to escape it. Says nothing about putting on more than I can bear.

Did I make the wrong decision? Forgiving him? Was I supposed to divorce him? Is that what this is about?

I'm alone.

No one has been through anything like this.

Yeah, I'm alone.

Nobody understands. Nobody can possibly feel what I'm feeling.

The door creaked.

"Jonetta," Michael said softly into the dark of the bedroom. Mom and Dad had brought me and the kids to their house. We'd made up beds in my old bedroom. That door had squeaked for years.

"I'm here," I said softly in return. He groped through the darkness toward my chair.

"Whew, you smell bad!" I said to his silhouette.

"I'm getting in the shower. How were the boys?"

"Shook up but okay, I think."

He squatted by the chair and wrapped me in a hug.

"They think it started in the kitchen. Jonetta?"

I'd passed out. The scoreboard of life, at that moment, read:

Exhaustion (1) | Jonetta (0)

Chapter 17

The Pay

I am a strong woman because a strong woman raised me.

—Leuk's widow

"Looks like a total loss," said the insurance adjuster after exiting what remained of our home. "We'll get you a check for living expenses–"

"When?" I interrupted without any concern for social graces.

He hesitated. "Middle of next week–"

"I don't think so," I interrupted a second time. "Let me tell you what you *are* going to do. You're gonna have a check ready first thing Monday morning–"

"Mrs. Shank, we can't–" he tried to insert.

"No, you listen to me. These clothes on our backs are the only things we have to our names, so don't you dare think for one minute that I'm gonna let you put us off or schedule us around your tee times – you get what I'm telling you, mister?"

"Yes, yes, Mrs. Shank, calm down–"

"You did not just tell me to calm down!" I was screaming at him as he waived his hands, palms facing down.

"Okay, I shouldn't have said – okay, how about 9:00 Monday morning? 9:00, is that okay?" he said in a scramble to diffuse my temper. He was smarter than he looked.

"Not a minute past," I chopped at him with my words, replying with terse disgust. Our insurance salesmen had been incredibly pushy; yet, this adjuster's attitude of open indifference during our time of need was more than I could take.

We stood in the driveway as the insurance man drove away, tail between his legs. The fire marshal was finishing inside the charred shell.

"Mr. Shank," he said exiting through a hole that used to be our back door. He was carrying something black. That was a poor choice of words. Everything in that house had turned black.

"Yes, sir," we turned.

"I'm real sorry folks, but it wasn't electrical." He held up the thing in his hand. It was my iron skillet.

"Ma'am, looks like it started at the stove, best I can tell. Grease fire. Had you been cooking something?" He looked at me.

"Oh my god!" I gasped and turned to Michael.

"Don't worry about it," he said firmly.

"I turned that burner off," I said. The words came slowly.

"What were you cooking, Mrs. Shank?" asked the marshal.

"Bacon…" my mind reeled. "I'd been frying bacon for a sandwich… Michael's blood sugar was low… he wouldn't make it to the restaurant… I turned off the burner and closed the door… he'd started the car… the boys were in the car…" I was talking out loud, detailing the events of the previous evening step by step. It felt like being in in a trance. Grief and frustration rose up from my stomach as I visualized what I had done.

"Honey, it's alright–" Michael was saying when the fire marshal interrupted again.

"Ma'am, it happens. Just glad nobody got hurt," he encouraged. I couldn't speak. Michael shook the man's hand and thanked him. The kind man got in his truck and pulled away as I stood there holding the twisted iron skillet covered in char, Michael's arm around my back.

A short time later Mom made lunch while I fed Paul. Andrew ran through the house swinging a plastic sword. I could hear Michael on the phone with Eddie, our sponsor in the business, and his tone wasn't good. He hung up without a "goodbye".

Lord, what now?

"What is it?" I asked when he came into the kitchen.

"Eddie," he said.

"What's wrong?"

"It's a scam," he said low, so mom wouldn't hear. I could see his anger.

"Mom, care if we got out to the front porch?" I asked.

"No, of course not. Go on, but lunch is almost ready," she said cheerfully.

We moved the conversation to the porch.

"What'd he say?"

"Eddie said that we'll start getting a nice monthly check," Michael said with sarcasm.

"But that's good – that's what we're working toward–"

"No, sweetheart, it's not," he interrupted. "He said we'll be getting a *secret* bonus since we've reached the direct level."

"*Secret* bonus?" I was confused.

"Yeah. He said we'll be making money off the books and tapes that everyone under us buys. Can you believe that? The organization demands that we listen to these tapes and buy these motivational books – stuff we can't afford to grow our business, and people are making kickbacks on this stuff! All the way up the line!"

Life can really kick the crap out of you when you're down. Problems seemed to be raining down without an end in sight.

"Michael, this is so wrong," I said with yet another heart-break.

"Yeah, baby, it is very wrong. Jonetta, we can't stay in this thing if this is how they're making money," he said firmly.

"You're right. What do we tell our group?" We had somewhere between 130 to 150 people in the organization we'd worked so hard to build.

"The truth," he said.

"But Eddie won't want that information to get out, will he?" I knew the answer.

"Jonetta," Michael said as he stood from the porch chair, "I don't care what Eddie wants at this point."

"Sit back down for a minute," not wanting him to end the conversation before I asked one last question."

"Okay, what?" he asked.

"Is that smoke I smell on you from being up at the house or is it cigarettes?"

Michael's face fell, then a grin crept across his face.

"Nothing gets by you, little woman," he admitted.

"Why would you go back to that, Michael," I asked sincerely. It wasn't a nag.

"Stress," he said quickly.

"You think that's gonna help–"

"No, it's not," he interrupted. He was irritated. I wanted to chew on him but knew it wouldn't do any good.

"Do what you want," I told him, and he heard the disgust in my tone. "But not in the house!"

"No problem – wasn't thinking of smoking in the house. Think we've got enough smoke in the–"

"Don't you even dare–" I wanted to tear into him for the cheap shot.

"Jonetta, Jonetta, I'm sorry," he said as he came to where I sat. "I didn't mean that–" he tried.

"Why would you say that to me–" I went on the attack.

"Listen, I was trying to make a joke and thought you'd laugh. It was a stupid thing to say. I'm sorry," Michael said with sincerity.

"Honey, I'm sorry, too. My nerves have about had it," I admitted.

I bathed the boys around 7:30pm. They'd been playing with their daddy throughout the evening and were now engaged in our bedtime routine. I had to keep their lives as normal as possible.

"Can I help?" Michael asked as I bent over the tub.

"No, I'm fine. Just finishing up. We're going to get a snack, then these guys are going to bed."

"No, bed, momma!" Paul protested with a splash of water.

"Yes, Pauly, you've got to go to bed," I said with a half-smile, half-stern look. He giggled.

"Then I'm going to town for a little while," Michael replied with a kiss on my cheek.

"To see who?" It was fear and anger.

"No one, Jonetta, I give you my word. I promise you, I just need to think and can't do it here," said Michael. It was the truth. Mom and dad's house was a continual turn-style of family in and out throughout the day and evening. Sisters, brothers, their wives, husbands and kids came and went.

Dozens had, from morning to evening, stopped in to see if we were okay. They'd brought clothes, food, toys, diapers, and toiletries of every kind. Their love and generosity surprised us. Word of house fires travel fast in small towns.

"I trust what you're telling me, just please don't make me regret it," I said with honest reserve.

"I'll earn it back," Michael replied. I knew he'd try.

Three years back in Illinois:

> *Job disappointments*
>
> *Financial despair*
>
> *Bankruptcy*
>
> *Spiritual starvation*
>
> *Loss of faith*
>
> *Workaholic entrepreneurialism*
>
> *No communication*
>
> *A dying marriage*
>
> *An affair*
>
> *Death of trust*
>
> *Loss of home: fire*
>
> *Loss of all belongings*
>
> *Giving up our business because of deception*
>
> *Loss of friendships*
>
> *Loss of dreams*

Living with my parents

He is smoking and drinking

Our life had been burning for years. Any hope that I had left was smoldering.

Jonetta Shank

Chapter 18

The Period

1994-2003

Do not judge my story by the chapter you walked in on.

—livelifehappy.com

It was 2003. Nine years had passed since the fire. Nine prosperous years of financial and material growth.

We had put new focus on our marriage and family after the fire and the departure of the network-marketing "pyramid" business. We'd experienced a renewal of love in our marriage that came from time together; time that had been stolen by the business.

Michael had achieved a pinnacle of success in two different fields. Our income was high, our home seemed happy, and the future looked bright.

Andrew was 13, Paul was 11 and Noah, our third son, was 3. I was pregnant with our fourth.

When 1994 ended in such chaos and catastrophe, life rebounded quickly toward the positive. Michael left the cellular business with a host of sales records in his wake to open a marketing company that specialized in air filtration and cleaning devices. He, without any surprise to me, set corporate sales records – all from that tiny southern Illinois community.

His career flourished as he moved deftly from one business to the next. He was, at his core, an entrepreneur who learned quickly and employed skill-sets I didn't know he possessed.

He pursued his education while operating the company, sold the business in late '99, then passed the Illinois Audiology boards, obtaining a license to become a clinician in Audiology.

He, just as he'd done before, exceled in the industry, opening hearing clinics in southern Illinois and Chicago. Michael dispensed and fitted record numbers of hearing aids to his patients. He won bonuses, awards, and all-expense-paid family vacations.

Our relationship seemed balanced. We enjoyed time together as a family. I worked hard to make our home a stable, peaceful environment for us all.

The great American dream was ours, but the money and achievements brought him no real happiness. He had returned to cigarettes during those dark moments in '94 as a crutch for the stress; it had turned into a pack-per-day addiction.

He'd also turned to alcohol. I hated alcohol, but he appeared to be able to moderate his drinking, so I tolerated it as best I could. We'd been through so much. Why rock the boat in times of peace and prosperity?

However, arguments were times of "war" and I intended to rock the boat in the heat of each battle. Our conflicts gave me opportunities to vent and rage about his drinking, but it didn't stop him. He seemed to drink more.

As his success grew, his drinking grew; as his drinking grew, my fear grew. I prayed for some type of intervention in Michael's life – something to show him that alcohol was a danger to him and his family.

Chapter 19

The Pathology

She was powerful, not because she wasn't scared but because she went on so strongly, despite her fear.

—Atticus

Christmas music played from a bookcase Bose system at one end of the spacious, elegantly decorated living room. The five of us laughed and talked over seasonal hors d' oeuvres chased with nutmeg flavored coffee.

Lisa was a consummate host, complete with charm and etiquette. Competitive joking from the kitchen volleyed over our conversation every few minutes – the men were engaged in an oyster eating contest. I could tell they'd had too much to drink.

"Jonetta, would you like more coffee?" Lisa reached for my cup.

"Oh, no, but thank you, Lisa. It sounds like it's time to put a bit in the horse's mouth." I smiled and stood. The ladies laughed in unison.

"Well, Jonetta, it's been a pleasure having y'all in our home this evening." Lisa hugged me lightly, not enough to admit any possibility of true friendship.

"Yes, thank you. We've enjoyed it," I replied.

The men abandoned their party as we filed into the foyer. Michael looked hammered.

Abe and Lisa were a couple who had been successful in the audiology industry, and some of Michael's associates. I didn't care much for either of them, pretentious as they were, but networking with Michael's contacts was important to him. And their annual Christmas party was a function, according to Michael, that shouldn't be missed. I'd decided it would be my last.

"Looks like you lost the contest," I said testily.

Michael laid his head backward on the headrest without saying a word. He'd learned to let me cool.

"Did you have a good time?" he broke the silence thirty minutes later.

"It was fine," I said with short, curt words.

"Why are you being… laconic?" he responded with a laugh.

"You're not funny, Michael," I replied.

"Yeah, but that Abe - he's a funny guy," he continued. "Lisa is a little snooty, though."

I pulled into our drive and turned off the car. "Let's talk tomorrow," I said as I walked quickly into the house... a house we had rebuilt after the fire, some nine years before.

Michael was up early the next morning making coffee... and ready to talk.

"Just tell me why," were my first words. No good-mornings, or hugs.

"Why what?" He looked genuinely confused.

"Why do you continue to drink like you did last night? You know I hate it and hate you when you drink! Just tell me why?"

He sat down at the table with his coffee and pondered the question. The crackle in his voice when he finally spoke alarmed me. I quickly looked at his face. Tears streamed down his cheeks.

"I don't think I can explain it, Jonetta," he said reluctantly.

"Would you at least try?" I gently asked. He rubbed the tears from his face with visible embarrassment.

"You're not the only one who hates me," he said with more strength.

"Honey, I don't hate you, I love you. I just hate who you become when you drink–"

"Well I hate me!" he interrupted.

"What do you mean?" I was surprised.

"I have some good news," he grinned.

"No, don't change the subject. What do you mean *you hate yourself?*"

The grin disappeared, and he seemed to close himself off.

"Michael, please just talk to me," I pled.

I waited through a long, uncomfortable silence.

"You know what I done to you years ago?" he managed to speak.

I knew what he referred to, but it was something that we tried not to bring up. Talk it out, resolve it, bury it and walk away.

"I think I know, yeah," I admitted.

"You forgave me, yes?" has asked.

"I *did* forgive you, Michael. Why are you bringing it up—"

"It can't be forgiven, Jonetta," he interrupted.

"Honey, I forgave you a long time ago—"

"No, Jonetta. I'm sorry. It's me. *I* can't forgive it." And he wept.

We talked from around 6:30am to about 10:00am, shutting down the conversation when Noah appeared sleepy eyed and hair standing all over his little head. He smiled at us both and ran to his daddy.

"I'm gonna pinch Sponge Bob," Michael said to Noah with a quick hug while playing pinching at his legs. Noah giggled and squealed in his raspy "not awake yet" morning voice. The older boys were still asleep. They milked Christmas break for all it was worth.

The morning talk had given me insight I'd never dreamed of. Michael's self-hatred and his inability to forgive himself was eating at him like a cancer. He admitted, to my horror, that he had experimented with marijuana and cocaine – anything to escape the relentless gnawing by the guilt he felt in his heart. Not only did the illicit drugs not help, the fact that he'd tried them caused increase to his feeling of guilt. He clung to alcohol because it worked, temporarily.

As I considered his feelings of shame and self-loathing, I listened to his thoughts about his faith, resentments, and regrets.

The accusations he leveled at himself were self-destructive and sabotaged a possibility for forgiveness. Did the accusations come strictly from his own mind, or did he have help?

It made me wonder about what I'd read in Revelation, chapter 12:

And I heard a loud voice saying in heaven, now is come salvation, and strength, and the kingdom of our God, and the power of his Christ: for the accuser of our brethren is cast down, which accused them before our God day and night (v.10).

It is written that the Adversary accuses the brethren before God and does it day and night. What is he accusing us of? It has to be our sins. Our disobedience. He accuses us of those things which we can't forget.

Michael didn't seem to need any help in that department. He accused himself day and night, his conscience branded continuously with a hot iron.

Moving back to southern Illinois had been the catalyst of our spiritual decline. How I wished we had considered the book of James when we were living in that little Bellevue apartment.

Go to now, ye that say, today or to morrow we will go into such a city, and continue there a year, and buy and sell, and get gain: Whereas ye know not what shall be on the morrow. For what is your life? It is even a vapour, that appeareth for a little time, and then vanisheth away. For that ye ought to say, If the Lord will, we shall live, and do this, or that. But now ye rejoice in your boastings: all such rejoicing is evil (Jas. 4:13-16).

The church at Bellevue had served as our spiritual life-line. We'd been so enthusiastic and evangelistic, naïve in our knowledge of the world, but living on a complete trust in Jesus Christ and His gospel.

It was a great life filled with a new baby, the best of friends, excellent jobs, and a bright future. A future we walked away from, with an ignorant assumption that we were strong enough to survive.

When we fell into financial suffering, our spiritual immaturity in combination with improper expectations planted a seed in Michael's mind that took root: the thought that God didn't care and no longer desired any involvement in our lives. The thoughts and perceptions were clearly wrong, but seemed valid in young, spiritually immature minds.

Discouragement and resentment followed. We fell into a spiritual death-spiral. His drive to make the pyramid business succeed pulled him farther away from faith and family. When it was found to be a scam, his resentment deepened, pulling us further downward.

The chasm in our marriage combined with his present spiritual discouragement opened the door to sin. He stepped through that door, shaking his fist at what he perceived to be a god who didn't care for him or his family.

Michael was tempted, drawn away by his own lust and selfishness. And, as James said, when lust hath conceived, it brought forth sin. And sin, when it is finished, bringeth forth death.

The soul that sinneth shall surely die. Is that exclusive to eternal destruction after our physical death, or might it have a tangent affect on our soul in the here and now?

Sin has an affect on the human psyche that is pathological. Sin creates a guilt that supersedes verbal admonishment. That guilt, if not dealt with accordingly, can and will destroy the quality of life during this time on earth.

Sin is a wound upon the mind and heart. Scars remain after the wounds heal, and it's these scars that become so difficult to live with.

Sin-scars impede spiritual health. They are constant reminders of things we want desperately to forget but cannot because of the nature of the scar: a reminder of the sin.

People try to cope with their scars through a plethora of unscriptural mechanisms, drugs and alcohol being a common coping method. These become avenues of self-sabotage and self-destruction.

When the user of alcohol sobers, not only do their sin-scars remain, they often find that they have new self-inflicted wounds caused during their drunkenness. It is a dangerous progression that many do not survive.

When the user uses long enough, addiction forms. Addiction removes the users free-will, which is the essence of addiction. The addicted loses their power to choose.

"Just stop! Put it down! Walk away!" Things easy to say, but impossible to do for the addict. Addiction is a whole new ball game.

Michael was on that path and I couldn't stop it. It was a helpless, gut-wrenching thing to watch the life of your loved one rushing headlong into a thing that will, most certainly, kill them, and feeling as though there's nothing you can do to prevent it.

Many will ask, "Why didn't you go back to church? Wasn't there a local congregation? How could you have been so stupid?" Simple shame. We lived in a small town and Michael's drinking had become known by the brethren. We tried to visit periodically, but shame overwhelmed us.

Michael's problem, as strange as this is going to sound, was not alcohol. His problem was guilt. Alcohol was a coping method – a vehicle of escape. It would turn into addiction if something wasn't done, and that would be a set of challenges that I knew we couldn't survive.

It's curious to note how we who believe in God view consumptive sins (i.e. alcohol, drugs, food, sugar, medicines). We say, "Don't look, don't eat, don't touch," while, seemingly, ignoring the root problem.

Consider symptoms as compared to diseases. According to most physicians, when a known hypoglycemic patient presents weakness, dizziness and irritableness, they need glucose in the form of fast-acting carbohydrates.

When a patient presents a yellowing of the sclera (white part of the eyeball), it's usually an indicator of elevated bilirubin in the blood (jaundice), so the liver is the first suspect.

When someone presents dramatic changes in personality, speech patterns and motor control, it indicates a potential problem in the frontal and temporal nodes – a neurological problem. In other words, problems and pathologies at a core, invisible level typically present surface problems which can be seen and observed.

Consumptive sins, in my experience, have been largely the result of a deeper, underlying pathology. In Michael's case, alcohol was a symptom of his underlying guilt. This is (or was), in no way, a justification or excuse for his behavior, but coming to the knowledge of his personal guilt and witnessing his self-destructive hatred called for more than the casual, "Drinking is a sin so don't do it" response.

Michael had sought alcohol as a form of self-medication and escape from guilt. He also used anabolic steroids. Michael was 5'10" and a hundred and twenty-five pounds when we married – just fifteen pounds heavier than me, and I was only 5'1". I loved him and didn't give his skinny frame a second thought, but his size made him feel weak and inferior: a Napoleon Complex. His insecurity caused him to compensate.

When a "gym" friend introduced him to injectable steroids in 1995, it was a quick fix for his body issues. Nothing I did was going to stop him. He went to the gym six days each week and gained over thirty pounds of muscle in a few months. Thank God his steroid use was short lived.

Michael had achieved his dreams: marriage, children, a high income, his own business, confidence, he was in great physical shape, but happiness eluded him – always just beyond reach.

My mistake? I saw many as I reflected over the past nine years. I had built my derrick, tapped into the potential of our marriage and our future, had learned how to help my man become a thoroughbred who provided a secure future to me and our children, and who loved me, but I had stopped praying when life turned toward the positive. It had been like taking an antibiotic – I had stopped at the first signs of feeling better. What a stupid and selfish thing.

Give a child what they ask for only to watch them turn away without any long-term appreciation or accountability. When God gave us increase, how did I respond? Did his answer to my prayers increase my prayer life, Bible study, or my desire to worship? I am ashamed to admit that I did the opposite.

Life had quickly turned around, back at a time when I couldn't take more pain and tragedy. Now, nine years later, every aspect of our lives had been blessed, and I went along as if the credit belonged to us.

Our socio-economic rise brought new prestige and influence in our small community. We relished new friendships with the "power-people" in town. Our boys enjoyed preferential treatment at school — tokens of advantage given only to the children of the community's affluent.

Dropping off and picking up the boys in a new Lexus amplified our materialism to envious onlookers. Calls and requests from the "popular" moms who ran most every school event now wanted me in their club. Me and my new rich-mom girlfriends prissed, pranced, gossiped and fake-faced at every school function.

I was miserable. It wasn't me. This life of money, influence, and materialism was a shallow lie. No wonder the rich-moms opened their wine bottles at 10:00a.m. I hated alcohol but could see the temptations of escape. My new "friends" were women who I secretly despised. They were spiritually, mentally, and emotionally about as deep as a bowl of jello. I judged them harshly and that judgment became a mirror of self.

It represented all that was the lust of the eyes, the lust of the flesh, and the pride of life. I had left Jesus Christ to follow the world, and life was a miserably hollow existence.

Here we were, nine years after experiencing such horrible life events. Nine years beyond what we thought had been our "bottom". Nine years of labor and struggle to reach what we'd both perceived to be the "top" of the social order. Three great kids with a fourth coming in the Spring, a beautiful home, self-employed, a big income, status, influence, popularity, travel, security and comfort.

But we were spiritually dead, and Michael's dependence on alcohol grew daily. Both of us were dissatisfied with the shallowness and vanity of our lives. Solomon said, "I have seen all the works that are done under the sun; and, behold, all is vanity and vexation of spirit (Ecclesiastes 1:14)."

Could I possibly turn this around? Again? But turn it around to what? We were now in our mid-thirties and had reached what was supposed to have been the American dream.

I knew in my heart of hearts what was missing, but didn't know how to go back. I had to repent – to examine myself, once again, in an honest effort to turn away from the sins I'd allowed to enter into my life. The trust and faith in our money had replaced my willingness to trust Him for our every need. My love and desire for material things had blinded me to life's true happiness found in a life of service. My lust for social status and influence had poisoned my humility and caused me to see the worst in everyone around me. And all of these worked in combination toward fueling my motivation to push my thoroughbred to win the race. I had allowed my horse entry onto the wrong track.

Dear Father, I repent of all of these horrible things! I will stop the madness and sins of lust and pride. Please forgive me for such neglect. Please forgive me for leaving you. Father, please accept me back into your love. How do I change all of this? How will we ever be able to live in your will again?

I prayed sorrowfully, with deep regret. Prayer was the only thing that I could do – it was all that was left. Tears flowed as I pressed my face to the floor again. The story of the rich young ruler came to mind:

> *And, behold, one came and said unto him, Good Master, what good thing shall I do, that I may have eternal life? And he said unto him, "Why callest thou me good? There is none good but one, that is, God: but if thou wilt enter into life, keep the commandments." He saith unto him, "Which?" Jesus said, "Thou shalt do no murder, Thou shalt not commit adultery, Thou shalt not steal, Thou shalt not bear false witness, honor thy father and thy mother: and, thou shalt love thy neighbor as thyself."*
>
> *The young man saith unto him, "All these things have I kept from my youth up: what lack I yet?" Jesus said unto him, "If thou wilt be perfect, go and sell that thou*

hast, and give to the poor, and thou shalt have treasure in heaven: and come and follow me. But when the young man heard that saying, he went away sorrowful, for he had great possessions (Matt. 19:16-19)."

Dear God, not this, please! Years ago we went through so much, You already know that! Please give me the wisdom I do not possess. Help me change our lives back into what You want. If You are unwilling to help me, I have nothing left, no where to go, no where to turn..."

God had already begun to answer my prayers about Michael's growing dependence on alcohol, but He was also going to deal with *me*. He was going to show me how I had allowed money and materialism to replace the trust I'd once had in Him.

His answer was coming quickly and would be dressed in disguise.

Chapter 20

The Prestige

We can't be afraid of change. You may feel very secure in the pond that you are in, but if you never venture out of it, you will never know that there is such a thing as an ocean, a sea.

—Joy Bell C.

Michael's good news was the answer to my prayers, and the speed of the answer surprised me.

A friend from the past had relocated to Dallas, Texas, and was head-hunting my man. The job offer provided a potential quarter-million-per-year income, came with a huge brick home in an upscale neighborhood, and Michael would own the business after a year with a seven-figure annual income.

I've been praying for a different life. A life that would bring us back to God. Praying that God would cause Michael to stop drinking. This had to be the answer. We would move to a new life, find a church in Dallas, renew our faith, get back to a life of service, develop friendships with Christians. This year's income will be bigger. I'll decorate our new home in Dallas. Spare no expense. Trade the Lexus on a BMW. Yeah, Michael will finally get that BMW he's dreamed about since Nashville. God doesn't mind our materialism.

Remember how God's answers are, sometimes, dressed in disguise? Solomon's words would be proven again. *Pride goes before destruction, and a haughty spirit before a fall* (Prov. 16:18).

Chapter 21

The Penury

[**pen**-y*uh*-ree] **noun**:
1. extreme poverty; destitution
2. scarcity; dearth; inadequacy; insufficiency
3. Indigence, need, want[1]

Here's all you need to know about men and women: women are crazy, men are stupid. And the main reason women are crazy is that men are stupid.

—unknown

A few months later in Dallas, Texas: a moment of terror. The clear Texas night turned into a tempest. My world was crashing down around me. Our home, a luxury forty-eight hundred square foot suburban manor with five-star curb appeal was about to become a tomb of despair.

Light glimmered through the huge plantation windows illuminating an outline of the spacious island that divided the gourmet kitchen.

An almost two-thousand-dollar-per-month mortgage buys a lot of pain!

I hated this house. Yeah, it was beautiful. Four bedrooms, three and a half baths, twenty-foot ceilings in the entry. Floor to ceiling windows in every room covered by wooden plantation shutters.

Three of the bedrooms had their own bath and walk-in closet. Customized built-in refreshment bars. Two separate living rooms, a second-floor family room, and a huge fireplace.

An ornate staircase descended from an upper-entertainment area into a foyer surrounded by elegant tilework showcasing a French chandelier.

Bragging? Hardly. This place disgusted me. Everything about this place was a reminder of what I was not. I wanted to crush the whole thing.

This spectacular home was a place of nightmares... a fortress where young professionals hid their darkest secrets.

And a man who'd once been a good man was peering through the living room's interior shutters, using long draperies as cover. He watched two dark-clothed men work with haste.

Michael didn't know I watched him through the slightly opened bedroom door. He'd been a thoroughbred full of confidence and ambition. The move to Dallas was supposed to have been a better life.

Nostalgia filled my mind as I watched him through the darkness... we'd met when we were just sixteen. He, like a skinny little bronco, bucked and snorted and jumped. He had shown off for me, his bride-to-be.

The unmistakable sound of iron clanked heavily from the driveway, sending vibrations through the house. I was pulled from thought. The repo man's job was almost finished, and the car wasn't the only thing he'd take.

How had we returned to such financial despair despite a previous decade of prosperity and material growth?

The move to Dallas had been based on promises of buying into a well-established, growing company that was going to explode the industry. The opportunity offered so much, and Michael had done his due diligence.

The company's market-base was slammed by an innovation introduced from a competitor just three weeks after our move. Michael's new job destabilized rapidly as the company's stock tumbled overnight. We had invested our life savings into the company and had used our emergency cash for moving expenses. Michael's job, income, and future evaporated before our eyes.

Few things destroy like financial loss. Ambitious men measure personal identity by financial gain or loss. My husband was born of that breed.

The flatbed holding our Lexus revved its engine, then quickly disappeared into the Texas night.

He'd be in here in a second!

I ran to the bed and slipped under the covers, hoping he'd believe I was asleep. But he would also need me, and I longed to hold him tight.

"Everything will be alright," I'd tell him. *"Tomorrow will be a new day."*

Minutes passed. The chime from our alarm indicated he'd went into the garage.

"He's walking it off," I told myself as I put on my pajama bottoms. *"I'll go to him and we'll talk it out. Everything's gonna be okay."*

I scurried down the hall through the laundry. A strange feeling of doom enveloped me. Something was wrong. Very wrong.

Nausea filled my body. My head started to spin. What in the world was happening?

The laundry door leading to the garage didn't seal properly, letting leaks of light to pass from the garage.

He's in the garage but the lights are off?

Fear covered me.

Hurry!

I reached the door and slammed the lever.

The garage was dark.

Movement!

I swept my hand upward over the drywall trying desperately to find the switch.

Light filled the room and I saw him. Michael had been standing in the dark.

He stood facing the the big metal doors, his naked back toward me.

He's just out here thinking. He'd spent a hundred nights out in this garage, lost in thought.

My fears started to subside but caught when he didn't turn around to face me. That's when I saw the end of it peeking around his thigh…

Shotgun?

He's got his shotgun! Oh, God, was he going to–

Chapter 22

The Panic

A woman has got to love a bad man once or twice in her life to be thankful for a good one.

—Mae West

Adrenaline pumped, flooding my bloodstream. Weakness followed. I leaned against the doorframe to prevent falling to the concrete.

Equilibrium came back. I walked toward him, desperately fighting internal emotions.

"Michael, what are you doing out here this time of night?" He stood eerily still.

"Oh, I was just looking at this old gun," he managed to say through an almost unrecognizable voice.

The feeling of terror that coursed through my body brought me to the verge of collapse, but something, or some power outside of me, seemed to keep me upright.

Our future hinged upon the next few seconds…

God, help me help him!

An eternity passed in nanoseconds. I stepped close to him, reaching around his mid-section to pull his back against my face and front. I heard those funny words he'd said many times from our past: *you're a little bitty stick of dynamite!* But any power I'd felt previously was gone.

My boys. I could see their smiling faces. The sound of their laughs and the smell of their hair filled my senses.

But something else seemed present in that garage... something dark and ominous.

"Michael John." The words came from my mouth as nervous wobbled tones. "Why do you have that gun out of the case?"

Time froze.

Two wolves within the one man, his two names representing the dichotomy of our nature: good and evil. Yes, I'd loved this bad man who I knew had also been a good man.

It was every woman's nightmare.

We stood there at the cusp of complete destruction. My hopes and dreams, the need for love, communication, affection, our children's futures –

everything in my world was teetering at the edge of annihilation with little to no chance of return.

And herein lies the question: how did you get through it?

The answer is multifaceted, which I will share, but begins with the simple component: Hope.

Paul said of Abraham, *"Who against hope believed in hope, that he might become the father of many nations, according to that which was spoken, so shall thy seed be* (Rom. 4:18)."

Woman, your capacity to hope when your current situation is without hope is of paramount importance. We possess this remarkable ability to hope when hoping makes no sense at all! Our ability to mobilize hope when all hope is gone is not only extraordinary, it is a gift to us by the Creator. And, woman, it is this unique faculty that we force all boundaries of possibility.

It is this same unreasonable, illogical, insane quest – hoping so strongly that something better is going to happen, even when you know with all your being that it cannot and will not! That is hope against hope.

Stop for a moment and consider the facts: Michael would have pulled the trigger had I not entered the garage at that *perfect* moment.

If I had entered moments before, he would have waited until he knew, for certain, that I was asleep. On the other hand, if I had entered the garage one full second later than I did, the trigger would have been pulled.

So, was "perfect timing" luck? Coincidence?

Or, is it possible that something else works actively in the lives of a people who seek, who knock, who petition, who obey and submit their will to something or someone more powerful than themselves?

The ancient words of Esther might touch your heart:

For if thou altogether holdest thy peace at this time, then shall there enlargement and deliverance arise to the Jews from another place; but thou and thy father's house shall be destroyed: and who knoweth whether thou art come to the kingdom for such a time as this? (Est. 4:14)

"Who knows whether you've come to the kingdom for such a time as this?" Sister, you are not an inferior, second-class citizen. You were designed by Him as a fulfilment to your counterpart. Your part in His grand scheme is the brilliant, beautiful melody sang but sometimes unseen.

But will your role be recognized?

You see, you weren't created to do what men can do. You were created to do what men cannot do. You will find, within this exclusivity, your individuality that enhances both beauty and power.

How does this relate to hope?

Nothing else clears the mind vision more than peering into the eyes of death; therefore, when the foundation of all that you hope in and depend upon dissolves before your very eyes, your true footing comes into focus.

Hope is the fire that heats our every ability. It is that "thing" which allows us – beings who see the pressing needs of today – look toward a brighter future. Hope is the essence of faith, and faith begets the force of God for good. Yes, faith is substance of things hoped for (Heb. 11:1). In other words, hope visualizes and fosters expectation; expectation brings substance from the Divine into existence. It all begins with hope.

Time thawed. My mind, still froze in fear and confusion, thrashed in mental mud. I held him tighter...

Chapter 23

The Providence

Maybe home is nothing but two arms holding you tight when you're at your worst.

—Yara Bashraheel

This man had almost, just seconds before, committed suicide with the gun he now held in his hands.

Do something! Say something!

"Jonetta Rose," his voice interrupted my frantic thoughts.

At least he was talking. Tears filled my eyes. I tip-toed, reaching higher around him. Every fiber of my body trembled. *What's he going to do?*

He said something about being unworthy. My lips moved. Words came out, but the only thing I remember was a complete feeling of physical "numbness," like Novocain to the gums.

Throughout our marriage I had served him like every wife serves her man. I had walked the tightrope of "wife," always teetering between the loving cheerleader and leader by proxy.

I loved this man so much, and my love for him caused me to try to be his "everything." A loving, submissive wife; an unequivocal supporter for his every idea; a chef, a housekeeper, interior designer and decorator. I dressed him, helped manage his schedule, and loved him in private.

I was a proficient mother, to the best that I could tell; a no-nonsense mom working from life's daily list of to-dos' – dispensing all the love, affection and discipline I could muster at any given notice.

And between dirty diapers, fast dinners, never-ending piles of laundry and the putrid dust that I despise (dust that appears almost instantly after hitting it with a Swiffer), I was determined to shave my legs, paint my nails and bleach my gustache (girl mustache).

He needed coaching when he was down, a psychologist when he wanted to talk, and a mother when he was sick.

Men. They flex and strut and boast. They do it for and because of us.

And I thanked God for my life. He'd worked hard, played by the rules, and loved me despite my own flaws. We'd made a life together with the blessing of four beautiful boys.

My life flashed in my mind. I squeezed him tighter.

Oh, I ought to kill you for doing this to me!

I realized how frail he'd become as I squeezed him in that garage, wanting desperately for a better life.

God, please help me help him… help us all!

It was at that very moment that my world changed! Upended, as if a box were overturned. The lies of the world seemed to pour from me. A new sense of security and peace took over.

Cut the baby in half! I felt a slight smile as I searched my mind for the story:

Then came there two women, that were harlots, unto the king, and stood before him. And the one woman said, O my lord, I and this woman dwell in one house; and I was delivered of a child with her in the house. And it came to pass the third day after that I was delivered, that this woman was delivered also: and we were together; there was no stranger with us in the house, save we two in the house. And this woman's child died in the night; because she overlaid it. And she arose at midnight, and took my son from beside me, while thine handmaid slept, and laid it in her bosom, and laid her dead child in my bosom. And when I rose in the morning to give my child suck, behold, it was dead: but when I had considered it in the morning, behold, it was not my son, which I did bear. And the other woman said, Nay; but the living is my son, and the dead is thy son. And this said, no; but the dead is thy son, and the living is my son. Thus they spake before the king. Then said the king, The one saith, This is my son that liveth, and thy son is the dead: and the other saith, Nay; but thy son is the dead, and my son is the living. And the king said, Bring me a sword. And they brought a sword before the king. And the king said, Divide the living child in two, and give half to the one, and half to the other. Then spake the woman whose the living child was unto the king, for her bowels yearned upon her son, and she said, O my lord, give her the living child, and in no wise slay it. But the other said, Let it be neither mine nor thine, but divide it. Then the king answered and said, Give her the living child, and in no wise slay it: she is the mother thereof. And all Israel heard of the judgment which the king had judged; and they feared the king: for they saw that the wisdom of God was in him, to do judgment (1 Kin. 3:16-28).

This happened in milliseconds. I was again reminded that I must save what I loved. Did I trust the Lord enough to say, "Do what You will, just let him live,"?

The thought opposed everything in my being. It opposed the desire of my own momentary feelings and emotions. It opposed the desire of my will; my ability to emotionally manipulate, direct and persuade this man toward my own direction. It was submission.

Uncontrollable tears flowed down my cheeks. The realization of "giving up" was almost more than I could bear. I'd never given up! Those boys depended on their momma and giving up had never been an option.

My marriage, our life, and our future depended upon *us* – two people that had become one flesh. But I couldn't go on… again. We were broken in every way: martially, mentally, financially, socially, and spiritually. Even our health seemed, at times, on the brink. It was as if we had come to a state of absolute, complete exhaustion.

I confessed all of this to Him, just as I've done now to you, but not aloud, because words kill. I'd learned a long time ago that the elementary rhyme we learn, "Sticks and stones may break my bones, but words will never hurt me," was a lie.

Words have the power of life and death, and I wasn't about to speak those things to God out loud.

The words would have finished Michael, for sure, so I said them silently to God.

Lord, do what You will, just let him live.

How did I get through this horrible event in our life? I did it through realizing my need to submit to the one Lord of this creation.

Jonetta, you've said enough. Your words won't work. God's words might.

Immediately upon saying those silent words to God, and idea shot from my mouth.

"King David! Your sins don't equal David's sins, and God forgave him! Michael, do you remember at what moment God forgave him?"

"No," Michael replied weakly.

Strength came to my legs and arms. I twisted him around to look into his eyes.

"Don't you remember what Nathan said?" I implored! The shrill sound of metal-hitting-concrete reverberated through the garage. He had dropped the shotgun. My confidence grew.

"It's 2 Samuel 12:13! Michael, God will forgive you of your sins!"

Sister, I am not a Bible scholar. I do not claim to know His Word, nor would I ever infer that I've memorized many scriptures. I'm only sharing the recollection – thoughts that might have been said with help from the Lord.

Sister, how do we, women, overcome life's worst moments? By surrender. It makes no sense to the world. Surrender is seen as weakness – a relinquishment of power and dissolution of self will; yet, surrendering to God empowers us beyond belief! It's no joke.

Regardless of what horrible event brings us to this point, surrendering to Him invites His presence and intervention into our lives.

"For whosoever will save his life shall lose it: and whosoever will lose his life for my sake shall find it." For

many years I had sought to save my life. I'd fought for love and security and family and future. It was time to lose my life for Jesus Christ's sake. It was surrender. My attitude, desires, fears, lusts, insecurities, temper, pride, anger, resentment, vengeance – all of it must be given up.

Paul's words filled my soul. "He must increase, but I must decrease. I must decrease so that He can increase."

God had answered in a most dramatic way; an answer of crystal clarity never to be forgotten. I had assumed that Dallas would be God's answer to my prayers. I assumed that the move would cause us to return to God. My prayers had been answered. God was working through our suffering to bring us to sincere repentance so that our accumulation of sins, bad decisions, and selfishness could be addressed and forgiven.

God's answer of suffering had been dressed in the disguise of "Dallas opportunity." God knew what was necessary, and He knew that we would never suffer voluntarily.

So, what first appeared as opportunity was, in reality, the deepest suffering we'd ever known, and it reached its objective: sorrowfulness unto repentance giving way to surrender of self. It is the only human state of being whereby God has invitation and opportunity to step into your life.

When your world crashes down around you, what's your solution? A different life? Different man? Divorce? More money? New city? Better car? Nicer clothes?

Here's a secret: What we want or think we need is rarely what is best for us. We process from narrow reference points, often using limited information conflated with pain, emotion, and selfish desire.

Maybe this is one of the reasons for Jeremiah's statement, "The way of man is not in himself, that it is not in man who walks to direct his steps (Jer. 10:23)."

I surrendered my life and prayed that I would never leave Him again. I won't rewrite the intricate details from *When Shovels Break*, as it would be redundant and unoriginal; however, God's answer was brilliant.

Are you beginning to see how you "make it through"?

Chapter 24

The Provision

Women are made to be loved, not understood.

—Oscar Wilde

Sleeping in the following morning:

Someone tickling my feet? Kissing my feet?

I felt strong hands around my ankles and kicked fiercely from impulse, jerking to an upright position. Michael laughed at my response.

"Hey, you're gonna give a guy a black eye!" He joked.

"What are you doing?" I barked. He released me with another laugh. *His weird foot fetish. Something was different.*

I bounced from the bed's edge, remembering the previous night with nervous fear.

"Relax," he said as he moved to sit with me at the edge. I heard the boys laughing from the kitchen. The smell of bacon floated through our bedroom.

"You cooking breakfast?" I was shocked.

"Yeah, the boys are eating –"

"But how'd you get groceries?" Our account was at about seventy-three bucks, and there were no bacon or eggs in our fridge.

"Got a guy who's gonna to buy my shotgun," he said cheerfully. It was the same gun he'd held just a few hours before.

Another shock. Money! Such a rare and coveted resource at that point in our lives.

"Really?" I looked to his eyes, clamoring for good news.

"Yeah," Michael laughed. "Rich Gilprin texted me this morning. He'd heard me talking about it last week. Offered $250.00."

"When's he picking it up?" The words spilled forth like someone with Tourette Syndrome. Distasteful and uncontrollable. No excuse. Cash was survival.

"Half an hour," he replied. Then he kissed me on the forehead and went back to the kitchen. Michael was different… positive, magnetic.

Male confidence is compelling, isn't it? A necessary force for their success. Does it come from us, for us, or because of us? It didn't matter. His new confidence energized me.

Relief! When he's filled with confidence and calm, I have a feeling of security. When his confidence wanes, my feelings of fear grow.

Sister, this isn't insecurity, co-dependence, or a phycological disorder. It's the simple understanding that men must be grounded in the knowledge that we love, forgive, admire, and respect them. Our respect and admiration builds male confidence – they feed on it. Confidence breeds courage and courage is what they've got to have to do everything in life. Courage is the component required for a man to examine himself, to face his flaws and to fall on his face in prayer before God.

Woman, how do you overcome? You grasp victory in the bold step to give away what you desire most… control. Control given by you to your Creator is handing off what you cannot control to Him who can control all.

Chapter 25

The Pee

Men are amazing. I love the way they are. They're consistently little boys, and they need to be nurtured and loved. But at the same time, they need to feel like men.

—Krista Allen

Get 'em out of the skillet.

Fried hotdogs... again. Split down the center, burnt on the edges, curling like pig-tails.

Noon's warm breeze flowed gently through the open windows along the rear of the house. The three boys played in the back yard of our small corner lot. I needed to be able to hear them.

If I never smell another fried hotdog for the rest of my life, it'll be fine with me. But hotdogs and white beans had been getting us through.

Lane babbled from the bouncer.

"Noah, stop!" exclaimed Paul. I could see Paul and Andrew through the window. They were standing on the patio looking toward our side street – laughing hysterically.

"What's he doing?" I yelped toward the open window while walking quickly toward the patio door. Our boys usually watched over Noah like little mother hens, but I knew from their laughter that he was doing something he wasn't supposed to be doing.

"Mom, look!" they pointed and laughed, frozen in place. I stepped out onto the patio and scanned over our small, well-manicured backyard. The class and civility of our subdivision of big, tightly-packed homes had been disrupted.

"Noah!" I screamed, running toward him. He stood at the edge of our yard facing the street, his back to us. A bright yellow stream flowed in a perfect arch high over the sidewalk and into the street's edge. And, at the same time, a van filled with a family drove slowly by... all of them with the same look of shock and awe.

"Noah Matthew Shank," I yelled, grabbing his arm and yanking him toward the house. The impressive display shut off instantly.

"You put that little thing back in your pants! Don't you ever pee out here again, do you understand me?" I said through clinched teeth, pulling him toward the back door as fast as his little legs would carry him.

"Momma, I had to pee–,"

"Then you know to come into this house, young man.

"And you two boys," Paul and Andrew's laughter vanished, "had better not have put him up to this." They scrambled through the back door and off to the safety of their rooms.

After making Noah wash up, I sat him up on the kitchen counter for a talk. His big eyes filled with tears.

After a short discussion about looking like being raised in a barn, he wiped his eyes. His little arms squeezed around my neck in a tight hug.

"Okay, so you understand?" I released our hug and looked at his face.

"I understand, Momma," he said in a most mature way. Then a sheepish grin crept across his face.

"What?" I inquired, fighting back a smile.

"Did you see how far it went?"

We burst out in laughter. He was four and already had a strong sense of humor.

"Just remember, Noah, you come in the house to use the bathroom," I encouraged while pulling him from the counter. "And don't hold it until you have to go so bad."

Noah walked toward his room and, without turning around or missing a beat, said, "I got the biggest wiener in Texas, momma."

"You'd better knock that off!" I laughed and stomped my feet. He ran to his room giggling loudly the whole way.

Life slowly improved. Michael read a little more each day, and I praised him for the smallest positives. The male ego and the power of words.

Chapter 26

The Patience

Tell the negative committee that meets inside your head to sit down and shut up.

—Ann Bradford

"Yeah, okay, Michael. It's a little strange."

He was venting frustration. The boys were busy swimming in the subdivision's community pool while we talked.

"But," I interrupted, "we can't base our faith on how they act." *Do I listen? How much is he going to take? Is he on the edge again?*

"Jonetta, it's been a month and nothing! No contact, no outreach, nothing."

He was talking about our attendance at a congregation close the house. The members were not what you'd call friendly. To make it worse, Michael had expected contact of some sort.

Expectations. His expectations are too high. He sets himself up for disappointment.

And what I wanted to do at that moment, more than anything else, was to join him in the negative banter. I wanted to vent and complain, confirming that he wasn't alone in his feelings. It would have felt like communication, but confirming his negativity would have, at that moment, been a mistake.

Women find love and understanding in communication, and when our man is on a soapbox – positive or negative, we want in. It's a response that intends, in most cases, to show understanding. Support for his cause. And oh, how I wanted to join this rant of his.

The past few weeks had been better in almost every way. He had sold two ATV's we owned but had left back in Illinois. The money was sustaining us while he looked for new work. But it wouldn't last long.

Michael was back to living in the moment. He was mentally present. We had a roof over our head and food to eat. We managed with one vehicle. He wasn't drinking. The boys were happy and safe, and I'd staved off another crisis (no, God staved it off with small assistance from myself). We were attending church, again. Worshipping, again. Trying to connect, again.

But I'd seen this coming. The congregation we attended wasn't a good fit. I knew it a few minutes into our first visit, but we knew of nowhere else. We just didn't know of another place to go.

"You think they have so many visitors they just can't get to all of them?" he questioned.

I measured his words, fighting the urge to criticize and complain. I wanted to show him support by talking about the unfriendly people, the lack of love, and the mind-numbing boredom I felt during service and sermons delivered by a passionless preacher.

I wanted to talk about the rudeness I'd seen there, and to laugh with him about that missing thank-you wave at our fist visit.

But sometimes this is the worst thing women can do. My participation in his negative thoughts would only affirm his feelings and cement his attitude.

Joining him in his rant was the easy thing to do, and it was the thing I wanted, but it would only hurt him. Staking-down his negative thoughts would serve to hurt all of us. This is a common mistake made by many women. Confusing communication with rallying negative attitudes.

"Maybe," I replied weakly. *God, help me. Our life is better than it's been in a long time. Please give me the wisdom to help us...*

"*Maybe* if you'd use deodorant the preacher and the elders might want to contact us," he said with a side-grin. He always made me laugh. The mental break in dialogue helped me to change gears. God seemed to help me with a thought.

"Honey, seriously," I brought him back to the issue, "let's keep doing what is right for us – for our family. Let's not make our faith about them," I replied.

Wow, where'd that come from? God's help in times of confusion and need continue to amaze.

Divine assistance is, in my life experience, a real and measurable truth, but only seen when looking back. It's visible only in the rear-view.

God's help during stress can be relied upon. Jordan Peterson (2017) said, "God has built into people [the ability] to deal with what they don't understand, which is a paradox. How do you deal with what you don't understand?" While we may never know *how* He does it, we see substantial evidence.

My response caused Michael to pause. He chewed on my suggestion, then his eyes sparkled.

"How about we try another congregation?" He said it as though it where some fantastic discovery.

And there it was. Words I'd been waiting for – words I'd been praying for.

Finally! Don't let him see your excitement.

"Where do we go?" I asked.

Does he know of someplace else or will he need to look?

I had, just days earlier, taken the phone book from the junk-drawer and had placed it on our counter peninsula; the counter that separated the kitchen from the family room.

Maybe the thing would jump off the counter, slam him in the head and scream, "Find another New Testament church!"

The strange part is that the phone book remained on the counter. We both hated clutter, so I was positive that he'd put it back in the drawer. It was a little surprising that he'd left it where I'd put it.

Michael was at a decision: find another congregation or forget church, faith, and God. We needed to find another congregation, of course, but he had to come to the idea on his own. His idea; his solution.

Sure, I could have suggested finding another church during the previous weeks (and had often bit my tongue), but Michael was trying his best to self-correct. He needed to stand on his feet again as a man, husband, and father. He was reading and praying, trying to prove his sincerity to God.

Michael stood up from the couch as he held Lane in his arms. Lane didn't wake.

"What is it?" I stood to take the baby.

"He's pooped," Michael said with a sour expression.

"Take him, would you? I need the phonebook," he said as he handed Lane to me.

Michael is getting the phone book! He's going to find another congregation! Thank you, Father. Thank you!

His reach for the phonebook might seem trivial, but it was, in reality, a huge moment in our life that represented a rebirth and renewal of spiritual alignment.

Only a fool says that there is no God, and only fools say that women have no power. Alice Walker, an American novelist and activist, said, "The most common way women give up their power is by thinking that they don't have any." Sometimes *we* are fools.

Chapter 27

The Paradox

A happy marriage is about three things: memories of togetherness, forgiveness of mistakes, and a promise to never give up on each other.

—Surabhi Surendra

We found a new congregation, developed new friendships, and regained purpose in purity. Michael turned away from every evil in his life in direct proportion to his desire for a good relationship with God (I pray you don't miss this powerful key).

I didn't push but, instead, increased my visible respect and admiration for him. His growth caused my respect to grow, and he made the connection without me saying a word (another powerful key).

Every aspect of our marriage and family life changed quickly and in the greatest ways. Our home had a new sense of peace and direction.

Our suffering had been paradoxical: fear, stress, and events that brought us to complete brokenness; yet, brokenness was the requirement of returning to God. The prodigal son's story.

How had our marriage survived? There was, as you've seen, no "one magic bullet". Both of us wanted to quit so many times throughout our marriage. Luckily, or more so by the grace of God, we'd never both wanted to quit at the same time.

Kim George, an American author, said, "Behind every happy couple lies two people who have fought hard to overcome all obstacles and interference to be that way [happy]. Why? Because it's what they wanted."

Woman, you were conjoined with your husband into one flesh by the mystery of God. It is a union worth fighting for and fighting through. Someone said, "Don't worry when I fight with you, worry when I stop, because stopping means there's nothing left to fight for."

Christ's words of Revelation are, in my opinion, the profound promise that is a perfect metaphor of marriage: *"He who has an ear, let him hear what the Spirit says to the churches. To him who overcomes, I will give to eat from the tree of life, which is in the midst of the Paradise of God."*

What a beautiful pact. Christ spoke His vision to John, stating that those who overcome [sin, struggles, sufferings, persecutions, doubt, fear] would be given life never to be ended again by death. He spoke of spiritual faithfulness unto death, but a marital metaphor can be seen in this passage. He and she who overcomes every tragedy, difficulty, suffering, and struggle presented in and by marriage will be rewarded with a wonderful, stable, solid, satisfying marriage filled with communication, affection, and a love deeper than you can possibly imagine.

God's original purpose for marriage between one man and one women was to join them into a singular and united flesh; a functioning living organism of two minds and hearts working in harmony toward common goals and dreams.

Such is Christ's relationship with His church. He called the church His "bride". He paid for His bride with His blood. She is His most valuable possession. She is His glory on earth and is the pillar and ground of the truth. She submits her will to His will and seeks to accomplish His goals in the face of sin and persecution.

He loves her with a perfect and complete love defined by the sacrifice of His own blood. He voluntarily gave His life for her; such should be a husband's love for his wife. Jesus modeled this kind of love which should be pursued and imitated by all mankind.

His love was never abusive or selfish. It didn't hold resentment and never kept score. His love sought all others before Himself and served selflessly at every opportunity. His love was extended to His enemies in quiet meekness, and His love was the most compassionate, understanding, and forgiving all.

I want you to take a moment to imagine this type of love in your marriage. It is a noble aspiration that you can experience in your marriage.

Michael and I have, as you've seen, clawed and scratched our way into this kind of love. Sister, I can say with all of my heart that it was worth it all.

Reaching this level of love takes work. You can't reach it by shortcuts. It's not quick or easy, and maybe this is why it's so valuable. Things that require little work have little value. If it was easy, everybody would reach it.

The entertainment industry loves to say, "Love shouldn't be this hard; love shouldn't be this much work; etc." The Hollywood lies being sown into each generation is producing a harvest of never-before-seen divorce rates, shallow relationships, and a people who are no longer willing to work for their marriage.

2004 was ending, and we were realizing that we needed to leave Dallas. There was only one place to go… southern Illinois.

Any move had to be approved by the Lord, and the designation must have a solid congregation of His people – a place where we could fit, sustain, and grow.

As I've said previously, When Shovels Break details our return from Dallas to southern Illinois, so I won't bore you with redundancy. I will, instead, show you a power hidden deep within you.

Chapter 28

The Provocateur

And the tongue is a fire, a world of iniquity: so is the tongue among our members, that it defileth the whole body, and setteth on fire the course of nature; and it is set on fire of hell.

—James, servant of God and the Lord

It is my hope that you will be enriched, empowered, and blessed by the things you're going to find in the following chapters, as they are the things rarely discussed in depth. I'm going to share powerful insights I've garnered over more than three decades of marriage – tools of knowledge that have brought me to a greater depth of love, happiness, and security.

Young or old, newly wedded or married decades, you should find the following to be practical, and immediately employable in your relationship.

Being a teenager in the '80's came with a fear that overshadowed much of life: The Cold War. My freshman physical science class spent the entire '81-'82 year on the topic of nuclear war. We covered everything from ICBM (Intercontinental Ballistic Missile) distances and destructive capabilities to building backyard fallout shelters.

We all knew that Russia had their vodka-soaked finger on the button, ready to start WWIII at any moment. When they did, the only thing to expect was mutual, total, and assured destruction – according to the political doctrine of the time.

One thought gave our generation solace. It was the hope that the super-power's nuclear arsenals were heavily protected.

Woman, you have something more terrifyingly destructive in you and more dangerous than a nuclear warhead – something able to destroy your world faster than a missile speeding to a continent.

You know full well what it is. It's your tongue. A dangerous tongue in the silo of the mouth, protected by nothing more than teeth and lips.

Yes, in your world your tongue can be a nuclear bomb that destroys everything around you in an instant.

In contrast, it can also be a miracle cure for the worst of life's plagues. Death and life hinge upon how and when your tongue is used.

Michael was giving a talk several years ago and used an analogy to illustrate the power and context of words. It was a story that I'll never forget. He was discussing this topic in front of a large group of married couples when he asked one of the men for permission to use the man's wife as a role-play assistant. The man laughed and said, "Of course."

Michael thanked the man and turned to the woman, asking her if she would be willing to help assist him in the task. She smiled and cautiously agreed. Michael took the woman's hand, looked at her intently and said, "When I look into your eyes, time stands still." The group was uncomfortably quiet.

"Ladies, if your husband said these words to you in this way, how would it make you feel?" The group responded positively, commenting that the words and intent would be a touching compliment, demonstrating thoughts of her beauty and magnetism.

"Alright," Michael got their attention. "I'm going to say the same thing, but this time using different words." He turned back to the woman and said, "Lady, you've got a face that'd stop a clock!" The room erupted with laughter.

"Ladies, how would *that* make you feel?"

Mutually assured destruction starts with words; words before anything else. Behavioral response is secondary. This begs the question, "How do we guard our tongue?" Do we guard it at all?

Today's movement of female empowerment feeds a constant diet that says we are to say what is on our mind and that any consequence of that action should be eliminated. "Speak your mind; be bold; lay down the law; say what you think; be the boss." And all these statements are made under the guise, "We are just being our 'authentic self'."

While I completely agree with telling the truth, I admit one of my biggest challenges is controlling my tongue. Sometimes I lack verbal diplomacy, and the consequences have taught me about the power of the tongue and its effects on relationships.

Your tongue is possibly your greatest and most detrimental power. God said we must guard this power and use it expeditiously (this goes for men, too).

Words are far more powerful than our thoughts and feelings because they, once spoken, can't be retrieved. Like trying to unring a bell, or gathering feathers thrown into the wind, we can't get them back.

The power of our words affect today and tomorrow. Words are the instruments by which we build or destroy, heal or wound, live or die.

Words reveal the thoughts of our heart. This idea is best seen in our children. One hot summer day Lane and I stopped at the post office. I had pulled into a tight spot between two cars and had put my SUV into park. Lane sat in his his car-seat behind the front passenger's seat with his window down while I thumbed through mail. He'd played with the electric window button until his window was fully open.

A young woman wearing a tight, very short mini-skirt, big hair and three pounds of makeup walked in front of our vehicle and around to her car door, which happened to be right next to Lane's open window.

"Hello, Ho!" He said too loudly through the open window to her as if greeting a new friend. I almost broke an arm trying to find the up-button, telling him to shut up repeatedly in a panic of embarrassment. Children don't realize the power of their tongues.

Are women the only ones who need to control their tongues? Of course not, but I encourage you to begin with that which you control.

Controlling the tongue requires true repentance, practice, and constant awareness.

Randall introduced us to an old-time preacher many years ago by the name of Don Rudd. Don preached in a way that I'd never heard. He said something during one of his lessons that I'll never forget. He said that it was easy for people to believe in the death, burial, and resurrection of Jesus Christ. He said the hard part was getting them to repent. He said that most people who read the Bible see the need to be baptized, but true repentance was an almost impossible task for folks.

Die to yourself. Die to your desires, your ways of doing things, and your will. Repentance. Cessation from a self-centered existence leading to the submission of our own will, turning our will over to His will is painfully difficult. I thought that I'd repented years ago, but age and experience was teaching me that needed to reach deeper toward repentance.

The Christian life is a daily quest: examine self, find the spots, clean them off. You can, when clean, encourage and assist others in their quest toward the same.

Chapter 29

The Prohibitive

There's fire in her. If loved correctly, she will warm your home; if abused, she'll burn it down.

—unknown

"Should I stay with a man who hits me?"

Michael has never hit me or physically abused me, so it's difficult to fully empathize, but I can certainly sympathize. I can only imagine the emotional devastation that accompanies physical abuse.

Many have emailed with this valid question, "Should I stay with a man who hits me?"

I have never personally heard of a kind, loving, respectful (to her husband) woman who is arbitrarily beaten by her husband, except for women in the Islamic faith and Hollywood movies. I am, of course, well aware of domestic violence and abuse. I've read the newspapers, magazines, and websites, along with the many videos discussing and documenting physical abuse in marriages across the world. There's no excuse for violence within marriage.

The premise at the core of our faith is love for all, love and prayers for our enemy, and the replication of Christ's passiveness combined with love to the point of enduring all violence without response. So, without sounding as though I am marginalizing the issue, or over-simplifying it, men and women need Jesus Christ. When one chooses to live within Christ, both in belief and practice, the initiation or response of violence as an option is removed, without question or dispute.

Now, sister, that's not to say that if Michael choose to hit me, I wouldn't hit back. He'd be lucky to survive! And if I couldn't fight back, well… he'd had to sleep sometime, right?

Our difficulties in coming to the right responses stem from the disagreement between our human nature and the teachings of Christ. This is to say that our faith requires love; love does not strike out or strike back, yet we want to strike back when struck.

The Romans beat Jesus mercilessly. The crowds spat at Him, they accused and railed against

Him, and ultimately murdered Him in a most hideous form of punishment.

Jesus had all power, and in that power showed the world the Divine manifestation of absolute love. His love is sometimes difficult to replicate, especially to those who are hurting us.

Additionally, there are factors that seem common in many domestic violence reports, such as drugs and alcohol. Alcohol is an anxiolytic[1] in moderate doses, but also acts to facilitate aggression in males[2] at levels differing with the individual. Alcohol reduces social anxiety and inhibition while increasing the response to agitation, known as the provocative response threshold (PRT).

A common scenario plays out in the following way: a man drinks to the point of PRT activation. His wife angrily confronts him for drinking or drinking too much. The confrontation escalates toward violence, many times because of alcohol on individual PRTs.

However, all the "science" in the world doesn't excuse violence. Should she, in this scenario, have been angry? Absolutely. Should she have confronted him while he was intoxicated? That's an unwise woman. A man full of alcohol cannot be reasonable, and there's a high likelihood that he will behave unreasonably and irrationally. Drunks often regret their drunken actions when they sober up, which is one of the many proofs that alcohol impairs judgement.

Solomon wrote, *"Wine is a mocker, beer is a brawler, and whoever staggers because of them is not wise* (Pro. 20:1)." Alcohol, or beer in this context, is a: combatant, opponent, aggressor, antagonist, battler, belligerent, bruiser, bully, contender, disputant, pugilist, scrapper, and slugger.

Isaiah said, *"In my hearing the Lord of hosts said, 'Truly, many houses shall be desolate, great and beautiful ones, without inhabitant. For ten acres of vineyard shall yield one bath, and a homer of seed shall yield one and a homer of seed shall yield one ephah. Woe to those who rise early in the morning, that they may follow intoxicating drink; who continue until night, till wine inflames them* (Isa. 5:9-12, *NKJV*)!'" Alcohol might be responsible for the destruction of more families and more homes than we could imagine.

Some argue that the Bible tells us to drink, citing Proverbs 31:6-7:

> *Give strong drink to him who is perishing, and wine to those who are bitter of heart. Let him drink and forget his poverty, and remember his misery no more* (NKJV).

I am not going to debate God's Word regarding alcohol and all its evils or purposes. I've got more reasons to despise it than most others, by my feelings and biases should not and do not bend truth. I share these things only for your knowledge and encouragement. If alcohol is lending to any kind of neglect or abuse, it is better to build a future free from it's destructive potential. For those who choose not to abstain completely, remember Paul's words, *"Let your moderation be known unto all men. The Lord is at hand* (Phi. 4:5)."

If a woman finds herself in a physically abusive marriage, God never said that she is required to cohabitate under the same roof. The same Paul said, *"But now I have written unto you not to keep company, if any man that is called a brother be a fornicator, or covetous, or an idolater, or a railer, or a drunkard, or an extortioner; with such an one no not to eat* (1 Cor. 5:11)." Your husband is also your brother if both he and you are in Christ, and Paul said not to keep company with any man called a brother who practices those specific behaviors. While physical abuse isn't on the list, the spirit of the instruction is the same.

In other words, if a woman leaves (not divorces) her husband for a time because he is beating her, she removes her love, service and care from him to make him see his behavior. It is an attempt to affect positive change.

Friend, if your man beats you, God never said you had to tolerate it, nor did He say you had to live under the same roof.

Again, begins with looking inside. We must examine ourselves. If your respect and dignified surrender doesn't transform the heart of your man, he might be beyond repair.

It's a process requiring more than faith alone. It begins with being brutally honest with yourself, trusting the Lord enough to apply His prescriptions, and examining the outcome so that you can come to a wise answer to the original question.

And for my litigious readers, I strongly recommend anyone dealing with abuse to seek professional help by a board certified professional specializing in marital counseling, and before it's too late.

(The previous sentence is not only good advice, it makes the lawyers happy when I write a qualifying statement that you should get "professional" help.)

Chapter 30

The Precursor

A happy marriage is the union of two good forgivers.

—unknown

There is a thing that men crave more than sex, and it's something often more difficult to give. It certainly requires more thought and discipline.

That thing is respect.

Respect from a woman is, believe it or not, like water or oxygen to a man. He cannot survive without it. Sadly, few women seem to know this relationship fundamental. Furthermore, many women don't know how men define respect in the way that respect is given to them by women.

Before we discuss a man's definition, we need to dispel an irrational concern: some fear that their offer of respect and dignified submission will turn their man into a disrespectful, domineering abuser (a useless and predatory male not worth his salt), but biblical respect does the complete opposite. God's prescriptive respect instills love and devotion in your man and creates a desire in him to lift you up, to protect you, and to care for you as the precious treasure you are.

A woman wants a man that will love her as his wife, protect her like she is his daughter, and respect us like his mother. We can't stand a spineless, mealy-mouthed male who's led by a ring in his nose. Unfortunately, some women might create this kind of man.

We want a man's man who hears, loves, and respects us. Yes, he must respect us, but we've got to give him something to resect (and vice versa).

Your gift of respect and admiration are transformational in efficacy. They act as meat tenderizers on the male heart.

When do we give him respect? Paul never said we get to determine if or when we give respect to our man. He didn't say that respect is given per our individual discretion, or contingent upon our current feelings and emotions. The offering is an act of personal faith, just as the step Peter took when walking over water toward Christ.

It's been said by counselors and psychologists that a vast proportion of infidelity stems from man's need for female admiration and respect. This is not an excuse for affairs, nor is it a defense, but the knowledge of what makes him tick is a powerful tool. The elements of respect and admiration, when applied properly with moderation and wisdom, do more to fix our man than almost any other behavior that we can offer. Our respect, as hard as it is to believe, has greater pull than sex.

How many times have you heard, "All men want is sex?" This is surprisingly untrue. Yes, boys want sex, and that's usually all they want, but mature men crave respect and admiration over sex almost unanimously.

Men will intentionally speak and behave in ways that make it appear as though sex is what they desire most, as the persona demonstrates masculinity, especially within groups. Men are fearful that any declination will be interpreted by the group as less masculine, resulting in a loss of position and respect, so they put sex in the forefront when engaging in male peer-groups.

If respect is more powerful than sex, and is something he can't survive without, what's his definition of respect? It's more complex than we'd like it to be, but easy to understand: show him in word and deed that he is superior to all other men.

If this sounds condescending, weak, or false, it's not – this is how you treated him when you were dating. It is why he married you above all others.

You made him *feel* as though no other man had a chance. You laughed at his horrible jokes and stupid behavior; you wore special outfits, made recipes you thought he would like and might showcase your skills, and you made time to say things that would draw him to you.

You made him *feel* like a god. You created in him a desire to love you, to want you, and to do for you. You criticized playfully but guarded serious judgements that would have risked damage to his ego.

You made him *feel* physically wanted, complimenting his strength or looks or characteristics or skills and talents. You mentioned his cologne or his biceps or his eyes. You played like a delicate damsel in need of a conquering knight.

You, through a culmination of words and deeds that defined your offer of female to male respect, captured his heart. You made him feel like a man in every way.

It is in this way that the adage finds its truth: a woman either let's a man be the man, or she doesn't. She has all power. A woman has power over him in two ways: the power of her respect and the power of her body. Sister, these are the two primary motivators of the male. You know it is true, and men will always try to live to your expectations, whether they be high or low, good or bad.

Wives, submit yourselves to your own husbands. Submission, in this context, is not as a slave, not as one who is inferior, and not as a doormat, but voluntarily giving to him what he craves the most. What should be received in return? His sincere love, his desire to protect you, his interest in listening to your thoughts and ideas, his motivation to provide for you, his drive to succeed for you, and his behavior of one who cherishes you.

We want to show respect to our man, but we often mistakenly expect him to be worthy of it before we give it. If we think he's not worthy, we revert to our default state of trying to fix him, shape him, and control him.

Sister, put a cart in front of a horse and you'll go nowhere. If you will exercise faith and respect him when he's not worthy (rather than using performance-based offerings), you will open his mind and heart. His attitude will become malleable to adjustment.

I've seen women disrespect their husbands without even realizing it, and in a host of ways. Here's a list of ways we disrespect him:

- Comments about other men (comparisons, attractiveness, strength, success)
- Talking about other men (why is another man on her mind?)
- Inordinate laughter at other men's jokes (reveals your attraction to another man; demonstration of flirting)
- Interrupting conversation (lack of interest or concern)
- Conversing with lackluster, indifference, or apathy
- Belittling (private or public)
- Demeaning publicly
- Criticize publicly
- Trying to manage his time, work, recreation
- Holding on to grudges
- Unwarranted questioning of his decisions
- Making decisions without his input or in his absence
- Dismissing or trivializing things that concern him
- Withholding intimacy or sex
- Using intimacy or sex as a tool

- Showing a lack of confidence in him

The male ego is extremely fragile and easily broken, and we hold more power than we know.

Women have mastered the art of identifying our man's faults and, when pointed out enough, create a relationship that is cold and distant.

Do you want to close that gap and bring back that closeness you once enjoyed? Do what you once did so well. Compliment your man. Compliment him every day. Do those things you did that made him feel like no other man has a chance, like he is wanted, and like he is a god (no, not God – you know what I mean).

Give, even when he doesn't deserve it, and the return will be priceless. This is a fundamental truth from the Divine; a complexity Paul called a *mystery*.

In turn your man will fall in love with you again. Truth be told, he'll grow to love you even more than he ever has.

Mignon McLaughlin said, "A successful marriage requires falling in love many times, and always with the same person."[1]

Chapter 31

The Picture

The most important thing a father can do for his children is to love their mother.

—Theodore Hesburgh

Sister, I love you for what you represent, for what you can achieve, and for the role given you by your Creator.

Being a woman is entangled with complexity, layered with responsibility, and christened in risk; yet, we were chosen from the marrow of man to accomplish all that he cannot, and to fit with him as the missing link.

Man was formed from the dirt of the ground, but woman from his unique bone. Consider that the Designer selected one bone from two hundred and six available, so why the rib?

It may have something to do with a possibility that the Creator used molecular DNA offered in the pre-packaged containers of cells found in red bone marrow. We've got to take a quick bite of anatomy, but it'll be short and sweet, like me [*joking*]:

I. Cells are needed to create life[1]

1) Bone marrow contains the best assortment of necessary stem cells for creating life

2) Bone marrow is red and yellow.

3) Red marrow contains two types of necessary stem cells:

    a. Hematopoietic (HSC): these create every kind of blood cell

    b. Stromal: these create bones, cartilage, fat and connective tissue.

II. Why the Rib Bone: Rich in Building Blocks

1) The rib and spine vertebra are rich in red marrow

2) Ribs offer easier and faster access to HSC's than do the spine, with lest risk and recovery time

3) The object is to harvest both hematopoietic and stromal cells (both necessary for the creation of life and

growth) without disturbing the medullary cavity[2]

4) The most easily obtained bone with no molestation of the medullary cavity is the rib bone [*Ibid*]

III. Why the Rib Bone: Regrowth

1) According to the National Scoliosis Foundation, the rib bone grows back in two to three months[3]

2) The new rib will completely harden and grow as strong as the original, providing the periosteum (membrane covering all bones) is left in tact [*Ibid*]

We are, in the past few years, finding out why God chose this bone from all those available in the body. Women, we are special, indeed. This fact proves the authenticity of our exceptional position, responsibility, and obligation to the betterment of family and society.

Today's women live in extraordinary times. More than ever before, we now have the freedom to pursue any career imaginable. However, remember that every decision comes with consequence.

I've been many things in my life, from accountant to business owner, but my life-long desire was motherhood. I wanted, more than anything else, to become the best mother possible according to my abilities. Raising a large family successfully was an ultimate goal that I saw modeled by my own mother. Her gift to me and sacrifices for me taught me the essence of love, the wisdom in discipline, and the value of forgiveness. I dare to say that there were none better in her chosen career path.

Motherhood is, at it's core, the transference of morality and values from one generation to the next

Motherhood is the creation, formation, and development of human beings, with the future success of her offspring contingent upon her success as mother – an exhaustive yet sublime evolution of teaching and learning.

Becoming pregnant is the easy part for most, but motherhood isn't for everyone. Those who find the demands and sacrifices of motherhood too demanding have no recourse, so count the costs.

The world needs great mothers, which is an outstanding reason for you to put every ounce of your energy and effort into developing a happy, rock-solid marriage. Raising children is hard enough within a good marriage, but much harder when you are a single parent, and evidential effects of the fatherless home are mind boggling.

If you are a single parent, this is not a judgement against you. It's my hope the Lord blesses you in the additional load you bear. I write these things as information and encouragement to all with the confidence that you would do the same, especially in light of your knowledge as a single parent.

Is a unified, two-parent home important? Here is a small sampling of statistics from *The Fatherless Generation*[4]:

- 63% of youth suicides are from fatherless homes (US Dept. Of Health/Census, 2018) – 5 times the average.

- 90% of all homeless and runaway children are from fatherless homes – 32 times the average.

- 85% of all children who show behavior disorders come from fatherless homes – 20 times the average. (Center for Disease Control, 2018)

- 71% of all high school dropouts come from fatherless homes – 9 times the average. (National Principals Association Report)

- 75% of all adolescent patients in chemical abuse centers come from fatherless homes – 10 times the average.

- 70% of youths in state-operated institutions come from fatherless homes – 9 times the average. (U.S. Dept. of Justice, Sept. 1988)

- 85% of all youths in prison come from fatherless homes – 20 times the average. (Fulton Co. Georgia, Texas Dept. of Correction)

- 71% of pregnant teenagers lack a father. [U.S. Department of Health and Human Services press release, Friday, March 26, 1999]

- 63% of youth suicides are from fatherless homes. [US D.H.H.S., Bureau of the Census]

- 90% of adolescent repeat arsonists live with only their mother. [Wray Herbert, "Dousing the Kindlers," Psychology Today, January 1985, p. 28]

- 85% of youths in prisons grew up in a fatherless home. [Fulton County Georgia jail populations, Texas Department of Corrections, 1992]

- Fatherless boys and girls are: twice as likely to drop out of high school; twice as likely to end up in jail; four times more likely to need help for emotional or behavioral problems. [US D.H.H.S. news release, March 26, 1999]

- Children who live absent their biological fathers are, on average, at least two to three times more likely to be poor, to use drugs, to experience educational, health, emotional and behavioral problems, to be victims of child abuse, and to engage in criminal behavior than their peers who live with their married, biological (or adoptive) parents.

Marta Lee said, "Your marriage is the backbone of your family. It needs to stay strong in order for your child to be happy, healthy, and to ensure the longevity and sturdiness of your family."[5] These statistics should, if nothing else has, open your eyes to the consequences of divorce upon your children and their future.

We don't live on an island whereby our choices affect only ourselves. Your choices carve pathways for your children, so choose wisely. Boyd K. Packer said, "Our whole social order could self destruct over the obsession with freedom disconnected from responsibility; where choice is imagined to be somehow independent of consequence."[6]

If this is the case, we all need help in learning how to have a happy marriage; learning how to have a happy, healthy, satisfying marriage is paramount to our future.

Chapter 32

The Paradise

Your spouse must never be a second, neither to family nor friends nor coworkers — not even to your children.

—unknown

Did you know that the tradition of wearing a wedding ring on the fourth finger from the thumb is because it is supposedly the only finger that has a vein which is directly connected to your heart?

Position of the ring doesn't mean as much as the position of your spouse. Put them before all others. Wear them on every finger. The position in which you place them is the beginning of happiness.

You and I need help with our marriage. We need to know what describes an ideal marriage, along with practical information we can use to get us there. We don't want shallow motivational anecdotes – we want the meat and potatoes for real living in the real world.

What is an ideal marriage? There are as many opinions as there are people, but everything begins with communication.

Jackie Bledsoe, author of *The 7 Rings of Marriage*[1], lists fifty of the most common responses to

his request that couples describe an ideal marriage in
one or two words:

1. Compromise
2. Dedication
3. Humor-filled
4. Christ-centered
5. Respectful
6. Godly
7. Safe
8. Effort
9. Acceptance
10. Great sex!
11. Patience
12. Perseverance
13. Silly
14. Loyalty
15. Dedication
16. Communication
17. Honest
18. Fun

19. God-ordained

20. Laughter

21. Kindness

22. Forgiving

23. Understanding

24. Passionate

25. Gracious

26. God

27. Friendship

28. Familiar

29. Relaxed

30. Faithfulness

31. Truth

32. Consistency

33. Love

34. Hope

35. Commitment

36. Sacrifice

37. Open-minded

38. God's love

39. Togetherness

40. Oneness

41. Best friends

42. Partnership

43. Self-awareness

44. Partners

45. God-sent

46. Blessed

47. Influential

48. Grace-filled

49. Caring

50. Serving

Are these good descriptions of an ideal marriage? They certainly are, but the better question is, "Can I achieve these in my marriage?" Absolutely. Can you implement these into your daily life? In theory, yes, but it takes a lot of time, effort, and continual focus. Would it be realistic to expect this "smorgasbord of paradise" every day? I'm laughing… sorry.

Look, we're intelligent women, right? Our idealistic nature desires all of these, but we live in a real world filled with suffering, struggle, and strife. There are days when life is good, other days when it's great, and days that are just awful.

Regarding percentages, is it correct to say that marriage is a 50/50 proposition? You can say it, but it doesn't make it true. The truth is that marriage is not 50/50. It's more like 90/10, 20/80, 40/40, 11/83 – all of which depends on the day, moods and emotions, life events, etc.

There are days when you feel like you're giving more than he is, and some days it will be the truth; however, consider the differences in male/female contributions when you feel the need to pencil in your scorecard.

You are two people tied together as one. You are trying to learn daily how to be individual, yet unified. It's a challenge, but the secret about the 50/50 proposition is simple: the only percentage that matters is that you will give 100% to keep your marriage together every single day until you die. It's a 100/100 proposition vowed by you when you married… the sacred 100.

Brides Magazine published an article in their August 2015 edition titled, "5 Wives Define What a 'Happy Marriage' Means to Them"[2]. The points are worth considering and sharing. They wrote:

A happy marriage is a cocktail of open communication, honesty, hard work, and a whole lotta love. But what does that look like in real life? Five wives open up about what a happy marriage means to them, because they're living it!

1. "A happy marriage is being happy with what you've got, rather than expecting your marriage to be a certain way," says one married woman. "Being content and grateful for what you have, instead of constantly trying to live up to some unrealistic standard set by movies and romance novels, is real happiness.

2. "In a happy marriage, two people share things equally," says another married woman. "It doesn't sound romantic, but I'm honestly happy because my husband does the dishes and the laundry as often as I do. We cook together, we run errands together. I don't feel burdened, and I don't feel taken for granted.

3. "We talk about everything, and I think that's what a happy marriage is," says one wife. "I've had relationships in which I felt like I had to keep secrets from my partner, but I can tell my husband anything. I like that I can be open about my feelings and know that we'll work through whatever it is together.

4. "This is my second marriage and it's happy, unlike the first, because we are totally honest with one another," says another woman. "Whether we aren't thrilled with what's happening in the bedroom or we're concerned over money, we spit it all out and then work it out.

5. "I think a happy marriage is about forgiveness," says another married woman. "No one is perfect and if you can just let go of the little things and move on from the bigger things, like arguments, with a forgiving rather than begrudging heart, you're in really good shape."

Dr. Chris Grace, Director of the Biola University Center for Marriage and Relationships, wrote an excellent piece on five qualities of a happy marriage in his article[3] of the same name:

Novelists, researchers, theologians and theorists from many fields—literature, psychology, communications, sociology—have long been exploring relationships. Over the past number of decades, people (and couples) who thrive, or struggle, or are somewhere in between, have been analyzed and studied from a variety of perspectives and approaches.

Marriage is one of the most reliable indicators of happiness. Martin Seligman writes in his book *Authentic Happiness* that "marriage is robustly related to happiness," is one of the best predictors of life satisfaction, and that married couples express the highest levels of happiness and satisfaction.

There is now much data to support the idea that happy people, and more specifically happy marriages, share common characteristics, such as:

Friendship: Happy, healthy marriages are marked by a deep and abiding friendship. Researcher John Gottman says that one observable sign of a healthy friendship and a happy marriage is seen in how they interact, finding that spouses nurture their friendships by demonstrating fondness and admiration, allowing the other to influence them, and creating detailed "love map" of their spouse's likes and dislikes (*Seven Principles for Making Marriage Work*). Happy marriages are marked by more positive then negative interactions, by a ratio of five upbeat positive interactions to every one negative interaction. And best of all, a deep and abiding friendship is strongly associated with couples highly satisfied with their levels of sex, romance and passion.

Togetherness: Neuropsychologists are exploring the idea that happy marriages and satisfying relationships are marked by a form of synchrony, a togetherness or "flow", with a matching of beliefs, values, ideas, humor, even body language movements that are literally in sync. Scott Stanley of the National Marriage Project finds that happy couples more frequently laugh together, confide in each other, work well on projects together, calmly discuss issues together, and rarely if ever discuss or consider divorce or separation. In fact, these "togetherness" traits are the characteristics used by researchers to define and measure the quality of one's marriage.

Affection: Happy marriages are marked by affection—mutual feelings of fondness or tenderness. Solomon's description of the affection felt between a couple in love is both poetic and instructive, showing us how to practice this passionate and companionate love. Affection is what C.S. Lewis in *The Four Loves* said, "is responsible for nine-tenths of whatever solid and durable happiness there is in our lives." Feelings and emotions are foundational in the pleasure and joy we experience in life.

"Other" focused: The apostle Paul, in a letter written to the early church in Philippi, said that caring for each other (Phi. 2:3-4) above one's own needs is the mark of a healthy relationship. For James (James 1:19) healthy relationships put into practice the notion of being quick to listen, slow to speak, and slow to get angry. These are signs of not only good communication patterns, but of an unselfish regard for the welfare of others. Many couples note with some sadness that the degree of their own selfishness became clearer as the honeymoon period faded and real life together commenced. Having biblical models to practice from has helped many couples find the joy in becoming more other-focused.

Shared spirituality: Happy couples create shared meaning with each other. A spiritually intimate marriage is one where a couple is prayerfully seeking after God in the innermost, sanctified places of connection that exist between a husband and a wife. Couples find spiritual closeness in a cherished affection for one another, found within a deep, abiding friendship and a romantic love, in a relationship centered on redemptive power of the gospel of Christ.

These five qualities—friendship, togetherness, affection, other-focused, and shared spirituality—are often found in the people who describe their marriages as "happy." These are the ways we love and desire to be loved—with a passionate, companionate, altruistic and spiritual love—manifested most profoundly in our affection, longing and love for others.

Sister, are you ready to see the meaning of the dream?

Chapter 33

The Paraphrase

Interpretation of the Phantasm (dream)

A woman's heart should be so hidden in God that a man has to seek Him just to find her.

—Maya Angelou

The dream was about a stallion in a grand stable, but it's so much more. If you don't remember the details, this is a good time to re-read chapter three and four.

Horses. We love 'em! It's no wonder that most young girls, at one point or another, dream of owning a pony, and why we, grown women, fantasize about riding through pine-covered mountains, or galloping down a sandy beach in warm summer sun.

Horses represent our need for mystery, romance, and enchantment. They cultivate dichotomous emotions of serenity and excitement. Horses are creations of God showcasing majesty and power, innocence inside beauty.

Their strength and speed are a combination offering great income through racing, companionship in daily life, and assistance in necessary labor. They can carry us and our load over diverse terrains and hostile climates with low maintenance.

They come in all shapes, sizes, and colors. Some are young, and some are old. Some are cowardly while others are bold. Some are strong, but others are weak; yet, some are unyielding while others are meek. There are fast horses and slow horses, work horses and show horses. Some are brilliant, and some are dumb, some have talents while others have none. Yeah, a poet and don't know it (laughing out loud)! Some horses mellow, but some will never be corralled.

Our relationship with them is symbiotic and delicate. A horse trainer once said, "If you wanna know how to have a good relationship with a horse, you've got to learn to live in their world using your brain and a couple of wise tools: a harness only when necessary but never long enough to break his spirit and love him when you ride. Don't yank him hard when you want to change directions, and don't ever abuse him. If he's carrying your butt, show him a little appreciation. You can walk in front of him with a whip, but you want him to have confidence in you, not your whip."[1]

The beautiful, majestic stallion in your dream is your man, and he wants one thing: to make you happy while retaining his position of respect and his desire to run.

Take time to learn. Learn for your benefit and for his. Learn what to feed him and how to feed him so that he comes to know that he can get these in none other than you. Learn your horse's unique personality and needs. Don't seek to be "equal" with him, as equality with your horse requires descension from your exquisite role to that of animalistic power and brute competition. Remember, again, that you weren't created to do what a horse *can* do – you were created to do what he *cannot* do.

Acknowledgement of this fact brings acceptance to your power and lifts you to a position of preference, protection, and adoration. This is where your horse, if he's a good horse, wants you to be.

The stable is your home, and you are the woman in the dream. When you were confused by the name plate pinned to her blouse, you were confused by the fact that the name was your name. You see it all from your point of view, but you are also *every* woman in the dream. Each role from great to small is a representation of an aspect of your life. They are everything in your life, from the mission-critical functions down to the menial, thankless things you do each day within your home. You are every servant to every professional in that stable. You, from poop-scooper to trainer, wear every hat – all being absolutely essential for success.

The stable Owner is God. He wants your happiness. He's given you the tools and methods to build and maintain it.

Sister, all of this begins with calling the office. It begins with sincere prayer. The Owner desires your contact, He appreciates your willingness to come to Him, and He will never leave you without the strength and wisdom you need to transform your life with your man, as long as it is something you truly desire.

Some ask, "To what end do we care for, encourage, convalesce, nurture, feed, and train our horse? Why am I doing this?" It's so that your horse can run and run to win in the race of life. It's a race we're all a part of, whether we want to be or not. Each is given a part to play and each part has been perfectly selected for their individual talents.

The key player in this great race of life is you, the jockey and trainer. Your value cannot be underestimated, and your contributions can't be overly emphasized. You provide everything within the stable and on the field. Solomon said, "Whoso findeth a wife findeth a good thing, and obtaineth favour of the Lord (Pro. 18:22)." The New King James renders the verse, "He who finds a wife finds a good thing, and obtains favor from the Lord (*Ibid*)."

If your man has you, he's found a measure of favor with God.

You want security, stability, and companionship. You want a man who listens to you and has a sincere interest in what you have to say. You want a man who will dream big but remember the little things in life, as well. You need a man who spends time with his kids, a man who provides for you and yours, and who will protect you with his life. You need a man you can trust. If your man has broken that trust, stop worrying. Trust is something that can be rebuilt, and it can be stronger than ever before. You can have an incredible life with your man, and I say this with confidence because my life is a living testament to this truth. Yes, what one woman can do, so too can you.

With all of this being said, it is time to open his deepest secret.

Chapter 34

The Power

His Deepest Secret

Man is the one who desires, woman the one who is the desired. This is the woman's entire but decisive advantage. Through man's passions nature has given man into woman's hands, and the woman who does not know how to make him her subject, her slave, her toy, and how to betray him with a smile in the end is not wise.

—Leopold Von SacherMasoch

What was your reason for coming here? Why did you invest your time and money in this book? What did you hope to find? Have you found what you where looking for? Have you seen something – maybe the smallest shred of a thought or an idea that hasn't previously crossed your mind? Have you been encouraged or emboldened? Do you know that the power to do all that you dream of doing is within you?

There is a deep secret within every man. It is his deepest desire – an inner craving he cannot locate. It is, somewhere in his mind and heart, a thing he cannot explain with words or actions.

His deepest desire is a primal need surpassing his drive for sex, success, and social dominance. It is on-par with his need for respect, and his drive for sex, yet it is something he can never discuss with you, or *anyone*. It is something that is so core to his being that it is too dangerous to speak of.

He knows that he cannot talk about this deepest desire with other men. Merely bringing it up would risk exposing some latent feminine crumb of his masculine character. Equally devastating is that it would expose him for being childish and intellectually immature. No, he could never and will never get close to revealing his inner desire with another man – not even someone he considers a brother.

And that doesn't matter, because he can't begin to describe his deepest need. He can, in rare moments of vulnerableness, point to it through uncomfortable phrases, as if he's found himself in a foreign city and trying with all his might to communicate with the few words of that language he'd heard in the past. His deep secret is elusive. He felt it when he was a boy, but it escaped him long ago. He's felt it since, but usually in small moments that passed so quickly that he thought it was only his imagination. He might have found it in someone else, but it didn't last; neither party knowing how it came nor how it went.

It is also something that is so elusive to him that it cannot be investigated properly, as an invisible wind that comes and goes. No one knows where it comes from or where it goes to or how it came to be. These are the many reasons why it remains a secret that has been almost impossible to understand.

His deepest desire is something that, if given, will fasten him so completely that escape is not an option. Therefore, great care and caution must be used in the knowledge of this secret. Remember that you, woman, take a heart into your hand. It is something that you have the power to protect and nurture, or to torture and destroy.

For a woman who can understand this deepest of all male secrets and, thus, give to her man this great gift, she will be the benefactor of a male loyalty beyond all imagination and understanding. She will become his greatest and most precious treasure – something that he will not be able to betray by his own volition or sell for any amount of riches.

His deepest secret need and desire above all others is a physical and emotional safe place that I call Protected Port, or port for short.

What is port exactly? Port is a place of complete physical and emotional protection created by you for him. Porting is your act of creating this place of complete physical and emotional safety, safe from every word and every thought. Port is where he has no chance of encountering criticism, complaint, advice, suggestion, talk, or judgment, so that he can peel off every piece of the shell that is his total self image: his male ego. He, in Port, is able to remove all male ego, but doing so requires a remarkable confidence in him. In other words, he must know without a shadow of a doubt that no potential pain will come from you. He must know that you won't put forth a single word, a question, even a facial expression – anything remotely negative will be put toward him from you. Woman, know this fact with certainly: one negative instance from you, whether a critical word or questioning expression, will destroy it forever, and Port is something that can never be rebuilt by the same women... ever. It is a one-shot, one-chance proposition. I will explain why you'll want to create Port and take this risk, but establishing his confidence is key. When he knows that there's no risk of potential harm from you, he will voluntarily remove all ego. He will temporarily, within the place of Port, set aside his suit of protection. It is a rare and remarkable occurrence to create a place whereby your man can be completely and totally vulnerable – a state of being so transparent that he could be easily and permanently destroyed. Your man is, in this place of Port, without defense.

Port gives him the rare opportunity to love you and to feel love from in a way that is pure and innocent, allowing him to love you unconditionally, because there is no risk to him. Port will return to you an unconditional love like you've never experienced in your life. As you establish his trust in your Port, the depth of his unconditional love will open to you. When he grows fully confident that your Port is impervious to anything that might harm him, he will give an unconditional love to you that is so incredible it cannot be explained; Port, therefore, can only be felt.

When you, woman, understand and believe my words, and take action to establish Protective Port for your man, you will bring your relationship to a level few women experience, and every woman dreams about. It takes time, effort, and patience, but worth everything you invest.

Woman, be careful who you choose to share this with, as some won't handle this knowledge with the best intentions or from a pure heart. Some will use this knowledge to seduce or manipulate, while others might use it to abuse someone emotionally. Whatever you do, use this information wisely and with care. Hearts are at stake.

Chapter 35

The Prescription

A woman is the full circle. Within her is the power to create, nurture, and transform.

—Diane Mariechild

Yes, we're living in the upside-down. Traditional marriage is being destroyed from every influential vantage point. If we openly embrace our Divinely appointed role with passion and exuberance, we're told that we are uneducated, oppressed sycophants.

Women are today, more than ever before, under attack by the very ones who want claim to speak for us. We're under a never-ending assault by the "enlightened" with their contemporary version of what we are supposed to be – completely sexualized, physically aggressive, immodestly dressed, stronger-than-any-male and fully autonomous of all male vestiges. The onslaught is a barrage intended to reshape societal perceptions and, thus, outcomes of female behavior. It is, sadly, working. And, ironically, the things that the "enlightened" are pushing are the very things which now destroy women at a speed and volume never before seen in human history. Women who subscribe to faith and traditional marriage are the primary threat to those who seek "modern transformation," and for those who raise their voices against radical ideology are labeled as intolerant fascists.

Women can certainly do what men can do, but it isn't about what men can do – it's about what men cannot do. It's about the knowledge and acceptance of our true power that is both unique and transformational. Buying into the contemporary mantras disguised as enlightenment is neither enlightened or beneficial to women, as doing so requires us to deny our unique potential, to voluntarily throw away our power, and to discard our latent capability to transform our selves and others. It is my opinion that the "enlightened" know this and is why they push with such tireless vigor.

Women have, by the fact of their gender, incredible power. Samuel Johnson, the 18th century writer and English literary critic, wrote, "Nature has given women so much power that the law has very wisely given them little,"[1] and his words record a profound truth few are brave enough to acknowledge. He wasn't kidding. We possess, through the Architect's grand design and masterful foreknowledge, a power that is unparalleled. This acknowledgement is further seen in Johnson's humorous statement, "Men know that women are an over-match for them, and therefore they choose the weakest or most ignorant. If they did not think so, they never could be afraid of women knowing as much as themselves." [2] Understand that Johnson was not degrading men as unintelligent or inferior. He was simply stating traits that are obvious in the most casual observation, and in the style of dry wit.

Use your power for good.

Do you have a man that needs to be fixed? Fix yourself first, then you might have a shot at fixing him. Are you struggling in a chaotic relationship? Throw away your scorecard, look at your faults before his, and open your heart to humility. Forgive all. Are you hopeless and without a future? Tell the negative committee in your mind to shut up and sit down. Then get down on your knees and pray. Ask for wisdom and strength. Focus on his best traits. Develop a vision for "what can be." Do you want more love and passion in your relationship? Apply some new-found respect and admiration, and you will have more passion than you can handle. Has communication disappeared from your marriage? Get your poisonous tongue under control. Demonstrate that you can listen with attention and speak without condemnation – communication will grow like a wildfire in a dry forest. He doesn't want to spend time with you? Be a fun friend rather than a strict mother, and you'll be shocked at his excitement the next time you ask him to go to the mall. Are there alcohol and/or drug problems in his life? Take the time to find the source of his guilt and self-hate. Does he resist coming home to you? What does your stable look and feel like? Is he a lazy couch-potato who seems unwilling to get into the race? Make him believe he's a race horse. Show him you have faith in him when he doesn't deserve your faith, and watch him rise to your expectations.

You have the power. You set the tone. He is the computer and you are the operator. You are his source of pain and pleasure, and you are the drive that motivates or the mouth that humiliates.

Woman, go and do as you choose. Do what you want. Do that which makes you happy, but remember that you never get to choose between "pain or painless" – life is pain, so choose the pain of discipline or the pain of regret. Those who seek the non-existent "third" choice of "painlessness" will live a life of insecurity, unhappiness, and fear; a hollow subsistence of fragmented relationships and painful discontent.

Woman, your life can become more than you've ever imagined, filled with love, passion, loyalty, security, companionship, contentment,

communication, affection, respect, admiration —
someone who will worship the ground you walk on.
You can have all of this and so much more, and you
can have it with your man. It's a decision away, but
everything you want is on the other side of fear. The
question is this: will you do what you must do to get
the life that is within your reach?

Chapter 36

The Plain

You must do the things you think you cannot do.

— Eleanor Roosevelt

Jonetta Shank

It's important to me that you understand my reasoning for writing this book. It wasn't for any potential "fame" or glory, nor did I expose my life and heart to you for any potential future profit. I wrote it, as you can see, from a heart-felt conviction that it might help someone struggling and suffering in the chaos of life.

My hope was that this true story might help one woman in need. If it ever accomplishes that aim, thanks be to God and Him alone.

There's a few things I didn't share in the story, but will share them now. Michael and I have both wanted to give up more times than we care to count. Fortunately, we never wanted to give up at the *same* time. Wanting to quit is a normal part of marriage. Feelings of love, whether "in love" or "out of love" ebb and flow throughout your relationship. A key to long-term success is making the decision to persevere through every struggle and pray that you both who't ever want to quit at the same time.

I've talked to scores of women over the past few years who are mothers, wives, daughters, sisters, and girlfriends – all wanting to know the same thing. "What's your secret to marital success? How'd you get through those really horrible things?" You've seen the "how to" in the story, but hopefully the "how not to" was an equally prevalent component.

Relationship repair doesn't take two. As a matter of fact, you'll fail if it's just you and him. In reality, it takes three. You, him, and God. This isn't intended to be preachy or overtly religious – it's just an immutable fact, and I'm not about to blow smoke or candy-coat for the sake of fearing being offensive. There's no amount of wisdom and instruction that can replace His prescriptive principles, but you know this within your heart of hearts.

I was blessed with a man who was sorrowful for his ways and wanted to mend our fractured relationship. I've been equally blessed to have been the daughter of parents who were married for sixty-two years. When mom died on May 2, 2015, it was left to me to tell dad that she was gone. I admit to you with complete sincerity that seeing his heart break upon hearing of mom's death was the worst experience of my life. Five days later he died. He died from a broken heart. The love of his life was gone, and he had no desire to remain in this world without her.

A remarkable number of people visiting their wake said, "That was the perfect example of marriage. That's how life is supposed to be. I hope to be that lucky." It was a double funeral and double burial.

That's the kind of love that you want. It's the kind of love I've always wanted, and I have that kind of love now. Reaching this kind of love isn't easy. It isn't without suffering and never without a fight, but I give you my word that it is will be worth your every effort.

You can have a wonderful home filled with love, excitement, and encouragement. You can create a stable home by creating a stable home (hope you enjoyed the play on words). There's no perfect man or woman, and remember that when leaving one man for the hope of another, you always bring yourself to every relationship. It's why I've put so much emphasis on you and self: yourself.

You are not the first to face the difficulties you are encountering, and you won't be the last, so muster a little faith and be strong. Go to the Creator – He is the beginning and end.

Smile in the face of stress, laugh at life, decide to be happy today, and be smart about picking your battles. Remember, if nothing else, the words of the ancient Persian poets, "This too shall pass."

Sister, here's your one shot at life. Choose to do it better today than you did yesterday. Don't be offended by my blunt nature. I am blunt to a fault. Yes, my mouth has gotten me into more trouble than anything else in life. Those of you who know me can personally attest to this fact. While Michael is gregarious and dynamic, I am introverted to an extreme. He enjoys meeting and greeting, but I am naturally opposed to those whom I don't know. Michael trusts everyone until they break his trust – I trust no once until they earn my trust. He sees the good in everyone (a trait I covet) while I am overly cautious, with a presumption that most are not inherently good and should be treated with caution. Michael and I are polar opposites that balance our relationship.

Michael is, in all honesty, one of the most talented public speakers I've ever seen, which is another reflective aspect of our opposite personalities. I do not and will not speak at anything – no women's events, women's days, public events, etc. There's a few things I have always refused to do, and public speaking is high on the list.

In the end I hope that my blunt tongue has given clarity to this story and effectiveness toward reaching your heart. May my plain speech be understood by any who reads this humble work. "*So also you, unless you utter by the tongue speech that is clear, how will it be known what is spoken? For you will be speaking into the air* (1 Cor. 14:9)."

Chapter 37

The Parroted

Wisdom and Humor

A strong woman looks a challenge in the eye and gives it a wink.

—Gina Carey

Here are some of my favorites quotes gathered throughout the years that have given me wisdom and a few smiles. I hope you enjoy them just as much.

Everyone must choose one of two pains: the pain of discipline or the pain of regret.

—Jim Rohn

~

What would men be without women? Scarce, sir... mighty scarce.

—Mark Twain

~

Sure, God created man before woman, but then you always make a rough draft before the final masterpiece.

—unknown

~

A male gynecologist is like an auto-mechanic who's never owned a car.

—Carrie Snow

~

As usual, there's a great woman behind every idiot.

—John Lennon

~

I hate to hear you talk about all women as if they were fine ladies instead of rational creatures. None of us want to be in calm waters all our lives.

—Jane Austen

~

No woman really wants a man to carry her off; she only wants him to want to do it.

—Elizabeth Peters

In politics, if you want anything said, ask a man. If you want anything done, ask a woman.

—Margaret Thatcher

~

I know enough to know that no woman should ever marry a man who hated his mother.

—Martha Gellhorn

~

Sometimes I wonder if men and women really suit each other. Perhaps they should live next door and just visit now and then.

—Katherine Hepburn

~

You only need one man to love you, but him to love you like a wildfire, crazy like the moon, always like tomorrow, sudden like an inhale and overcoming like the tides – only one man and all of this.

—C. Joybell C.

~

A man's face is his autobiography. A woman's face is her work of fiction.

—Oscar Wilde

~

Any fool knows men and women think differently at times, but the biggest difference is this... men forget, but never forgive; women forgive, but never forget.

—Robert Jordan

Women like silent men. They think they're listening.

—Marcel Achard

~

If you want the rainbow, you gotta put up with the rain.

—Dolly Parton

~

A great marriage is not when the perfect couple comes together. It is when an imperfect couple learns to enjoy their differences.

—Dave Meurer

~

Be kind to women. They constitute half the population and are mothers to the other have.

—unknown

~

Little girls with big dreams become big girls with vision.

—unknown

~

Things you don't want to realize too late:

- 90% of your happiness comes from your marriage/primary relationship.

- Choose wisely or choose to be unhappy.

- You're going to feel pain anyway; either the pain from growth or pain from regret. Choose growth.

- If you don't create a plan of execution for your goals and dreams, you'll probably never achieve them.

- Take intelligent risks; everything in life has risk – love, work, adventure – all of it. That's what makes life exciting and worth living.

- People love people who love themselves. People respond to your energy. If you feel worthy, so will they.

—Maria Consiglio

~

Strong women don't play the victim, don't make themselves look pitiful, and don't point fingers. They stand and deal.

—Mandy Hale

~

I choose to be kind because it makes me happy, but I will defend my boundaries and my loved ones without hesitation. Make no mistake – I am fierce.

—Nanes Hoffman

~

Be a girl with a mind, a woman with an attitude, and a lady with class.

—unknown

~

It's hard to be a woman: you must be tougher than a man, act always like a lady, have the appearance of a young princess, and work like a horse.

—unknown

~

You only live once, but if you do it right, once is enough.

—Mae West

~

There is no such thing as an ugly woman.

—Vincent Van Gogh

~

Women are always beautiful.

—Ville Valo

I was meant to be woman-the-joyous, but I carry in my heart a thousand centuries of pain. I was meant to be woman-the-radiant, but my eyes tell a world-old story... This destruction that we permit through our own unenlightenment, this gnarled and knotted being, this life bound to its pack, is not of God. It is of you, or it is of me. God gave us time to live, but we have so distorted it that we have only time to perish.

—Muriel Strode Lieberman

~

A woman can say more in a sigh than a man can say in a sermon.

—Arnold Haultain

~

If a woman has to choose between catching a fly ball and saving an infant's life, she will choose to save the infant's life without even considering if there are men on base.

—Dave Berry

~

I believe that women who are forced to choose between catching a fly ball and saving an infant's life will save the infant's life while catching the ball because she always knows who's on base. Men, it's called multi-tasking.

—Jonetta Shank
[included at Michael Shank's request]

~

Women cannot complain about men anymore until they start getting better taste in them.

—Bill Meher

Next to the wound, what women make best is the
bandage.
—Jules Barbey d'Aurevilly
~

Before a woman can advance, man must love her for the
higher, not the lower faculties of her being... the wife,
the friend, the mother.
—Henry James Slack
~

You start out happy that you have no hips or boobs. All
of the sudden you get them and it feels sloppy. Then,
just when you start liking them, they start drooping.
—Cindy Crawford
~

Every girl should use what Mother Nature gave her
before Father Time takes it away.
—Laurence J. Peter
~

Whatever women do they must do twice as well as men
to be thought half as good. Luckily, this is not difficult.
—Charlotte Whitton
~

The average woman would rather have beauty than
brains because the average man can see better than he
can think.
—unknown
~

Curve: the loveliest distance between two points.
—Mae West
~

A pessimist is a man who thinks all women are bad. An
optimist is a man who hopes they are.

—Chauncey Mitchell Depew

The two women exchanged the kind of glance women use when no knife is handy.

—Ellery Queen

~

Women get the last word in every argument. Anything a man says after that is the beginning of a new argument.

—unknown

~

The rarest thing in the world is a woman who is pleased with photographs of herself.

—Elizabeth Metcalf

~

Whether they give or refuse, it delights women just the same to have been asked.

—Ovid

~

However, I'm not denyin' the women are foolish: God Almighty made 'em to match the men.

—George Eliot, Adam Bede (Mrs. Poyser)

~

Women are like elephants to me. I like to look at them, but I wouldn't want to own one.

—W.C. Fields

~

Ah, women. They make the highs higher and the lows more frequent.

—Friedrich Wilhem Nietzsche

~

Women keep a special corner of their hearts for sins they have never committed.

—Cornelia Otis Skinner

Every woman is wrong until she cries, and then she is right – instantly.

—Sam Slick

~

I have an idea that the phrase "weaker sex" was coined by some woman to disarm some man she was preparing to overwhelm.

—Ogden Nash

~

When men reach their sixties and retire, they go to pieces. Women go right on cooking.

—Gail Sheehy

~

If women didn't exist, all the money in the world would have no meaning.

—Aristotle Onasis

~

Men will always delight in a woman whose voice is lined with velvet.

—Brendan Francis

~

They may talk of a comet, or a burning mountain, or some such bagatelle; but to me a modest woman, dressed out in all her finery, is the most tremendous object of the whole creation.

—Oliver Goldsmith

~

Men really prefer reasonably attractive women; they go after sensational ones to impress other men.

—Mignon McLaughlin

Women are never stronger than when they arm
themselves with their weakness.
—Marquise de Deffand

~

Women dress alike all over the world: they dress to be
annoying to other women.
—Elsa Schiaparelli

~

I married beneath me – all women do.
—Nancy Astor

~

Woman begins by resisting a man's advances and ends
by blocking his retreat.
—Oscar Wilde

~

I'd much rather be a woman than a man. Women can
cry, they can wear cute clothes, and they're the first to
be rescued off sinking ships.
—Gilda Radner

~

It is only rarely that one can see in a little boy the
promise of a man, but one can almost always see in a
little girl the threat of a woman.
—Alexandre Dumas

~

A woman wears her tears like jewelry.
—unknown

~

A woman's tears and kisses are her strongest
arguments.
—James Lendall Basford

Women are in league with each other, a secret
conspiracy of hearts and pheromones.
—Camilla Paglia

~

A woman should soften but not weaken a man.
—Sigmund Freud

~

I prefer the word homemaker, because housewife
implies that there may be a wife someplace else.
—Bella Adzug

~

Men enjoy being thought of as hunters, but are
generally too lazy to hunt. Women, on the other hand,
love to hunt, but would rather nobody knew it.
—Mignon McLaughlin

~

A man gives many question marks, however, a woman
is a whole mystery.
—Diana Sturm

~

The chief excitement in a woman's life is spotting
women who are fatter than she is.
—Helen Rowland

~

A man who thinks he's smarter than his wife clearly
does not know how smart his wife really is.
—Rush Limbaugh

~

God did it on purpose so that we may love you men
instead of laughing at you [this was in reply to a male
acquaintance who asked why women seemed to have
no sense of humor].
—Mrs. Patrick Campbell

And verily, a woman need know but one man well in order to understand all men; whereas, a man may know all women well and understand not one of them.
—Helen Rowland

~

The supply of good women far exceeds that of the men who deserve them.
—Robert Graves

~

A man is as good as he has to be, and a woman is as bad as she dares.
—Elbert Hubbard

~

You should never say anything to a woman that even remotely suggests that you think she's pregnant unless you can see an actual baby emerging from her at that moment.
—Dave Berry

~

Look like a girl, act like a lady, think like a man and work like a dog.
—Caroline K. Simon

~

A man chases a woman until she catches him.
—American Proverb

~

Beauty is the first present Nature gives to women, and the first it takes away.
—Méré

~

Brains are an asset, if you hide them.
—Mae West

Women speak two languages – one of which is verbal.
—William Shakespeare

~

Nature has given women so much power that the law
has very wisely given them little.
—Samuel Johnson

~

Fighting is essentially a masculine idea; a woman's
weapon is her tongue.
—Hermoine Gingold

~

Women worry about what men forget; men worry
about what women remember.
—unknown

~

The people I'm furious with are the women's
liberationists. They keep getting up on soapboxes and
proclaiming women are brighter than men. That's true,
but it should be kept quiet or it ruins the whole racket.
—Anita Loos

~

No matter how happily a woman may be married, it
always pleases her to discover that there is a nice man
who wishes that she were not.
—H.L. Mencken

~

W: Wonderful mother
O: Outstanding friend
M: Marvelous daughter
A: Adorable sister
N: Necessary to mankind

—unknown

Marriage is conflict, compromise, and negotiation toward the reward of fulfilling companionship, later reaching a depth of love rarely obtained outside its framework.

—Jonetta Shank

Chapter 38

The Practical

Wise Anecdotes

To be a woman is to be unapologetically resilient despite everything.

—H.H.

Practical knowledge can't be accurately valued by any known method, but the efficacy is evidentiary. Knowledge from life-experiences disseminated into subsequent generations, with repeating and predictable outcomes become self-supporting proofs.

In other words, practical advice is good stuff – read it, think about it, and apply a little of it to your life. Here's a few anecdotes and practical tidbits passed down from my parents and grandparents:

- The grass isn't greener – it's just a different shade of green.
- Don't let a desire for your 15 minutes of fame become an obsession – you'll be worse off in the end.
- Words once spoken are as feathers in the wind – you can never get them back.
- You can't un-ring a bell.
- What happens in Vegas ends up all over the internet.
- You give eternal life to anything you put onto the net; it will find you.
- Keep your personal life personal; Facebook is merciless.

- Ignore gossip, lies, falsehoods, slander, and the like; your response is the oxygen that those fires need to burn. It will suffocate in the absence of oxygen.

- There's two sides to every story.

- Be thankful for the good and the bad; always give credit to your Creator.

- Tragedy takes you to dark, lonely places; while you didn't choose to go there, you can choose not to make it a permanent residence.

- Avoid the poisons of life (tobacco, alcohol, drugs).

- Hold your head high and do the right thing.

- If you need to break down, do it at home; it's never forgotten if done in public.

- Accept advice from your parents – they know what they're talking about.

- Avoid negative people and those with bad habits; you become like those you associate with.

- Don't give advice about something you've never lived; you're not qualified.

- To say, "I know how you feel" is insulting; better to say, "I can understand why you would feel that way".

- Never discuss marital problems with family/friends; they're compelled to side with you and become frozen in time.

- A woman always knows what she looks like when she leaves the house; dress appropriately. The world is full of seductresses who excel in advertising.

- Respect yourself; behave in ways that demonstrate the respect you have for yourself.

- Think about what made you fall in love with him/her every day.

- Being loud-mouthed is a sign of low-breeding; behave in a way that would make your mother proud of you.

- Appreciate those who have raised you, as you'll never know the sum total of their sacrifices in doing so.

- Know when to say no.

- Be stronger inside than anyone expects. Being underestimated is a good thing.

- Under-promise and over-deliver.

- The best time to be kind and thoughtful is when you don't feel like being kind and thoughtful.

- It's true – misery loves company; if you're not miserable, the miserable will try to make you miserable. Don't join the party.
- Expect love to change – it's not all "puppy-dogs" and "rainbows"; those with endurance find that deep, meaningful, lasting love.
- Your kids know more than you think, see more than you know, and never forget your true self.
- Flesh and blood over "friends" because friends have no skin in the game.
- Don't let your kids do things that make you dislike them because they will turn into adults that nobody likes to be around.
- It's amazing how many "one child" parents want to give advice on raising "children".
- Let your kids be kids; they'll spend most of their lives being adults.
- Be "there" for your children, and for your parents.
- Live below your means; money doesn't grow on trees.

- You stand on your own two feet; the achievements of your ancestors is not a credit to your own talents or intelligence, nor are you responsible for their sins.
- No one is perfect; no one is blameless.
- How do you eat an elephant? One bite at a time.
- Rome wasn't built in a day; learn patience and persistence.
- Save money for a rainy day.
- Forgive and forget to the best of your ability.
- Never take the Lord's name in vain; He judges those that do.
- You can get through anything with your dignity in tact.
- There are two kinds of people: givers and users.
- There are two kinds of girls: "good-time" girls and the kind a man will marry.
- You "deserve" nothing other than life, liberty, and the pursuit of happiness.
- Celebrate the small things in life – they look much bigger as you get older.

- Withhold discipline from your children only if you don't love them. Your lack of discipline does them a great disservice.
- Learn to live in the moment; people who live with one foot in yesterday and the other foot in tomorrow are peeing all over today.
- Spending time with those you love is something you will never regret.
- Giving kids everything they want "spoils" them; what does society do with things that are spoiled?
- Pray every day.
- Never give up, never give up, never give up.
- Quitter's don't win; winners don't quit.
- Your lack of planning shouldn't constitute an emergency for others.
- Holding a grudge acts as a cancer.
- Pick your battles wisely; most things don't fall under the nuclear option.
- If you don't have anything nice to say, don't say anything at all – it's still the best advice.
- People can change. Most want to, but don't know how.

- Everyone deserves a second chance (and a 3rd, and a 4th, and a 5th...) as long as they are sincere, and trying, and sincerely trying.
- Learn to juggle... literally.
- Everything you say and do has a consequence and effect, even if only on you.
- Pick up a hobby, girls. Hobbies are a nice thing to do... once a year, or so.
- Don't be a needy or whiny – it's not attractive.
- When you're wrong, accept it. It won't be often, but it'll happen.
- The key to everything: communication.
- Your man is, by default, a fixer, which is why he finds it so confusing to talk to you. Which mode? "Fix it" or "just listen to me"? Be kind enough to tell him beforehand.
- Confrontation is a part of every marriage; learn to fight fair.
- Get your face out of your phone – life is passing you by.

- Stop busying yourself in the life of others; keep your nose in your own business and you'll have all that you can handle.
- Stop worrying about what the naysayers think.
- Social media is a weapon that destroys your ability to live in the moment.
- Stop trying to be a "friend" to your kids – they've got friends. Kid's need a parent much more than they need another friend.
- Don't give in to peer pressure... at any age.
- Yes, it's true – you can't make everybody happy; trying is futile, wasteful, and disappointing.
- And who can forget – don't take any wooden nickels (never knew what that meant).

ORDERING INFORMATION

You can get single copies at discounted pricing through our secure, direct-from-author page, as well as multi-copy volume discounts on all our products. Visit:

https://www.michaelshankministries.com

We hope you will like and follow us on Facebook.

OTHER PUBLICATIONS

- Muscle Trilogy: Muscle and a Shovel, When Shovels Break, Hope Against Hope

- Hope Against Hope paperback, hardback, Kindle, eBook
- Hope Against Hope 13-Week Student Workbook
- Hope Against Hope 13-Week Teacher's Manual

- Muscle and a Shovel paperback, hardback, Kindle, eBook and audio
- Muscle and a Shovel 13-Week Student Workbook
- Muscle and a Shovel 13-Week Teacher's Manual
- Muscle and a Shovel Spanish
- Muscle and a Shovel Portuguese
- Muscle and a Shovel Hungarian
- Muscle and a Shovel Russian

- When Shovels Break (sequel to Muscle and a Shovel) paperback, hardback, Kindle, eBook and audio
- When Shovels Break 13-Week Student Workbook
- When Shovels Break 13-Week Teacher's Manual

- Revel Knox: 7 Times from Hell paperback, Kindle and eBook (Western Fiction)
- Revel Knox: Singleton's Revenge (pending publication)

SCRIPTURAL REFERENCES

CHAPTER 1
Esther 4:14

CHAPTER 5
Jeremiah 10:23
2 Kings 5

CHAPTER 8
1 Timothy 6:9-10
Proverbs 20:24-30
Job 1:6
Matthew 16:23
1 John 3:8
2 Corinthians 2:11
Galatians 6:11
Genesis 3:1
2 Corinthians 11:14
2 Timothy 4:3
1 Timothy 4:1
2 Corinthians 2:11
Ephesians 6:11
2 Corinthians 11:3
1 Peter 5:8

CHAPTER 10
Matthew 5:19
Matthew 19:9

CHAPTER 11
Proverbs 5:3-5
Job

CHAPTER 12
Hebrews 11:6
Matthew 13:3-9
Jeremiah 31:34

CHAPTER 13
Ephesians 1:3
2 Corinthians 5:7

CHAPTER 14
2 Corinthians 13:5
Proverbs 29:18
Philippians 4:8
1 Peter 3:7
1 Peter 4:7
John 14:15
Psalm 34:17-19

CHAPTER 15
Proverbs 16:18
Psalm 10:4
Isaiah 2:12
Isaiah 23:9
Philippians 4:8
Ephesians 4:2
Colossians 3:12
James 4:10
James 4:6
Genesis 49:25

CHAPTER 19
Revelation 12:10
James 4:13-16
Ecclesiastes 1:14
Matthew 19:16-19

CHAPTER 20
Proverbs 16:18

CHAPTER 22
Romans 4:18
Esther 4:14

Hebrews 11:1

CHAPTER 23
1 Kings 3:16-28
2 Samuel 12:13
Jeremiah 10:23

CHAPTER 29
Proverbs 20:1
Isaiah 5:9-12
Proverbs 31:6-7
Philippians 4:5
1 Corinthians 5:11

CHAPTER 33
Proverbs 18:22

CHAPTER 36
1 Corinthians 14:9

QUICK REFERENCE TOPICAL INDEX

ANGER
Pro. 14:17, 14:29, 15:1-8, 16:32, 29:22

ASSURANCE
Heb. 6:11, 10:22
Col. 2:2

BACKSLIDING
Gal. 5:4, 6:1
1 Cor. 10:12
John 15:1-6, 17:11,15
Heb. 3:12-14
2 Tim. 4:2
Jas. 5:19-20
Luke 22:32
1 Thes. 5:14

CHILDREN
Gen. 33:5
Psa. 127:3
Pro. 1:8-9, 6:20-23, 13:24, 17:6, 22:6, 15, 23:13, 30:7
Deu. 6:6-7, 30:2, 31:12-13
1 Tim. 3:4, 5:4
2 Tim. 1:5, 3:2, 15
Eph. 6:1-4
Ecc. 12:1
Col. 3:20-21
Phi. 2:14-16
Mat. 28:19-20
Luke 2:51-52
Rom. 1:30
Mark 7:10-13

CONSCIENCE
Rom. 2:15, 1:9

2 Tim. 1:3
Heb. 13:18
1 Pet. 2:19, 3:6, 21
Acts 23:1
2 Cor. 1:12
1 Jo. 3:19-21

DISCIPLINE
1 Thes. 5:14
2 Thes. 3:15
Gal. 6:1

DARKNESS
Psa. 139:11-12
1 Cor. 4:5
Luke 12:3
Pro. 4:19
Ecc. 2:14
Eph. 6:12
1 Jo. 2:11

DECEIT
Pro. 24:28
Psa. 52:4
Rom. 3:13, 16:18
Tit. 3:3
2 Tim. 3:13
2 The. 2:10
2 Pet. 2:14
Mark 4:19, 7:22
Mat. 13:22
Gal. 6:3
Jas. 1:26
1 Cor. 3:18
1 Jo. 1:8

DIVORCE
Deu. 22:19; 24:1-4

Jer. 3:1,8
Isa. 50:1
Mal. 2:16
Mat. 1:19; 5:31-32; 19:6-9
Mark 10:2-12
Luke 16:18; 17:3-4
1 Cor. 7:10-15, 39
Eph. 5:33
Rom. 7:2-3
Heb. 13:4

DRUNKENNESS

Hos. 4:11
Eph. 5:18
Gal. 5:19-21
1 Cor. 6:10
Rom. 13:13
Pro. 20:1, 21:17, 23:21, 23:29-32
Isa. 28:7-8
Luke 21:34
Mat. 24:28-51

FAITH

Mat. 8:10, 17:20
Rom. 4:20-21, 5:1-15, 10:17, 14:1
1 Pet. 1:8
2 Pet. 1:1
1 Cor. 15:14
Jude 20
John 5:46-47
1 Jo. 5:4
Jas. 2:17,22
Gal. 5:6
1 Thes. 1:3, 3:10
Mark 11:22
Heb. 11:6, 13
Eph. 2:8
Acts 6:5, 11:24, 24:14

FAITHFULNESS
1 Cor. 1:9, 4:2, 10:13
2 Thes. 3:3
1 Jo. 1:9
1 Pet. 4:19
Rom. 3:4
1 Tim. 4:8-9
2 Tim. 2:2, 13
Tit. 2:10, 3:8
Luke 16:10-12, 19:17
Mat. 25:21

FALLING FROM GRACE
Jude 1
1 Pet. 1:5, 5:5-7
John 10:27-28
Rom. 8:12-13, 14:4
1 Cor. 10:13
Jas. 4:6
Heb. 3:12, 4:11
Gal. 6:7-9

FEAR
Pro. 8:13, 9:10, 12:13, 14:27, 16:6
Rev. 14:7
Heb. 12:28
Phi. 2:12
Eph. 5:21
Psa. 103:11, 13, 147:11
Acts 10:35
Exo. 20:20
1 Pet. 3:2

FORGIVENESS
Acts 3:19, 8:22, 10:38
Neh. 9:17
Dan. 9:9

Exo. 34:6-7
Isa. 43:25
Mic. 7:19
Col. 2:13, 3:13
1 Jo. 1:5-7,9
Jas. 31:34
Luke 6:36, 17:4, 23:34
Mark 11:25
Mat. 5:44, 6:14-15, 18:21-35
Eph. 4:32
1 Pet. 2:20-23
Pro. 19:11
Rom. 12:20

GRACE
1 Pet. 3:7, 4:10, 5:5, 10, 12
2 Pet. 3:18
2 Tim. 2:1
Jas. 4:6
Heb. 4:16, 10:29, 12:15, 28
Acts 4:33, 11:23, 20:24
Eph. 1:6-7, 2:7, 4:29
Tit. 2:11
1 Cor. 15:10
2 Cor. 6:1, 9:8, 14, 12:9
Rom. 5:15, 6:1, 14, 15
Jude 4
John 1:16
Gal. 2:21, 5:4
Col. 3:16, 4:6

HEART
Mat. 5:8, 6:21, 11:29, 12:34
Luke 6:45, 8:11-12, 15, 12:34, 21:14, 24:25
Mark 2:8, 7:21-23
Acts 2:37, 5:33,7:54,11:23
2 Cor. 9:7
John 14:1

Eph. 3:17
2 Chr. 19:3
Psa. 24:4, 34:18, 51:17, 112:7
Rom. 6:17

LOVE
1 Jo. 2:5, 3:14, 4:7-10, 12, 20
John 3:16,18, 14:15, 21, 24, 13:34-35
Luke 6:27-28, 7:42, 47, 10:22
Tit. 2:4
1 Pet. 1:22, 2:17
Gal. 5:13, 22
Col. 3:14
Rom. 5:8, 8:37, 12:9, 13:9-10, 14:5
Mat. 5:44-45, 6:24, 22:37-39
Eph. 2:4, 5:2, 15, 5:2, 25, 28, 33
2 Thes. 2:13
Heb. 6:10, 12:6
1 Cor. 13:4, 13, 14:1, 16:14
2 Cor. 2:8, 5:14

MEEKNESS
1 Tim. 6:11
2 Tim. 2:25
Col. 3:12
Jas. 1:21, 3:13
1 Pet. 3:1-4, 15
Gal. 5:23, 6:1

MAN
Gen. 1:27, 2:7
Mat. 10:28, 16:26, 22:32, 25:41
Gal. 3:26

MARRIAGE
Mat. 19:4-9
1 Cor. 5:13, 7:1-5, 9, 33-34, 39, 11:3
1 Tim. 5:14

Gen. 2:18-24, 3:16
Mal. 2:14
Heb. 13:4
Rom. 7:23
Eph. 5:22-29
Pro. 5:18
Col. 3:9, 18
1 Pet. 3:7
Tit. 2:5

PRAYER
1 Cor. 13:8
1 Jo. 3:22, 5:14-16
Mat. 5:44, 6:3,5- 8,11, 15, 18:21-35, 23:14, 26:39, 41
Luke 5:8, 6:28, 11:4, 18:1-8, 10-14, 11:42
Eph. 3:14
1 Tim. 1:5, 5:5
Psa. 119:105
Jas. 4:2-3, 5:16
John 3:22, 14:13, 15:7, 17:21
Heb. 4:14-16, 10:22, 11:6
Mark 11:24, 12:38-40. 13:33, 14:38
1 Thes. 3:10, 5:17
Col. 4:2
Phi. 4:6
1 Tim. 2:1

PRIDE
Pro. 6:16-17, 11;2, 15:5, 18, 18:12, 21:4, 29:23
Psa. 73:6
Mark 7:22-23
Oba. 3
Dan. 5:20
Luke 14:11, 18:11-12
1 Cor. 1:29, 31, 8:1, 13:4
1 Tim. 3:16
Mat. 23:12
Isa. 2:12, 13:11

Jas. 4:6
Gal. 5:26
Phi. 2:3
Rom. 3:27, 12:16
Eph. 2:8-9

REPENTANCE
2 Cor. 5:10, 7:10
Heb. 1:6, 12:17
Acts 2:38, 41, 3:26, 8;22, 36, 11:18, 16:33, 17;30, 26:20
Luke 5:32, 13:3, 15:7, 10, 17-19, 21, 24;46-47
Mat. 3:2, 7, 8, 12:4, 21:29
Rom. 2:4-5
1 Pet. 3:20
2 Pet. 3:9
Phi. 3:7-8
Mark 1:4, 14-15, 6: 12
2 Chr. 7:14
Jas. 4:9-10
Jon. 3:10
Eph. 4:22-24
Col. 3:5-10
1 Jo. 1:5-7
1 Thes. 1:9

REDEMPTION
Mat. 20:28
1 Tim. 2:6
Tit. 2:14
1 Cor. 1:30, 6:19-20, 7:23
Rom. 3:24, 6:18-22
1 Pet. 1:18-19
Rev. 1:5, 5:9
Eph. 1:7, 4:30
Col. 1:14
Gal. 4:5
Heb. 9:12

RICHES
Pro. 10:22, 11:4,28, 13:7, 14:24, 15:27, 21:6, 22:1-2, 16, 23:4-5, 27:24, 28:6, 20, 30:8-9
Mark 10:23-27
Rev. 2:9, 3:17
Hos. 2:8
Mat. 6:19-21, 13:22, 19:21
Heb. 13:5
Phi. 4:9, 11-12
Acts 20:35
2 Cor. 8:9
Eph. 2:7
Deu. 8:17-18, 25:13-16
1 Cor. 1:27, 2:2
Ecc. 5:19
Jas. 2:5
1 Tim. 6:17-19, 6:6-10
Amos 2:6-7, 5:11-12, 8:4-6
Joel 3:3
Lev. 19:36
Psa. 52:7
Luke 19:8, 12:13-21, 16:9-11, 18:22-23,

RIGHTEOUSNESS
Psa. 7:9, 14:3, 116:5
1 Jo. 2:29, 3:7
Rev. 16:5
Tit. 2:12, 3:7
John 17:25
1 Pet. 2:24
1 Tim. 6:11
2 Tim. 2:22, 4:8
Luke 1:74-75
Heb. 12:11
Eph. 5:9
Acts 17:31, 24:25
Phi. 1:11, 3:6-9

Jas. 3:18
Rom. 3:10,20,23, 24-28, 6:16, 18, 8:30
Gal. 2:16,21, 5:5
1 Cor. 1:29-31,
2 Cor. 5:21, 6:14
Mat. 5:6, 6:33,13:43

SPIRITUAL DEATH
Isa. 59:1-2
Eph. 2:1-2, 4:18
Col. 2:13
Luke 15:24, 32
Rom. 6:1-2, 16, 23, 8:6, 12-13
1 Tim. 5:6

SUFFERING
Rom. 2:4, 3:25
2 Pet. 3:9, 15
Col. 3:12
Eph. 4:2
2 Tim. 3:10
1 Thes. 5:14
1 Cor. 13:4
Gal. 5:22

SATAN
Job 1:6, 12
Mat. 4:3, 13:19, 16:23
Gen. 3:1, 6
Gal. 5:19-21
Pro. 27:20
Ecc. 5:10
Jas. 4:6-7
Eph. 6:10-12
1 Pet. 2:11, 5:8
Luke 4:1, 22:31-32
1 Jo. 2:14, 16, 3:12, 5:18-19
Rev. 12:3, 9, 20:2

John 8:44, 13:31, 14:30
2 Cor. 2:11, 4:4, 11:3, 14
Rom. 13:31, 13:14
Mark 4:15
Acts 5:3, 13:10
2 Thes. 2:10-12, 18

SELF CONTROL
Pro. 4:14-16, 23, 16:32
Acts 11:23, 24:25
2 Pet. 1:6
1 Cor.5:6, 9:25, 15:33
1 Tim. 5:22
2 Tim. 1:2, 5, 2:22, 3:15-17
1 Thes. 5:17
Col. 4:2
Mat. 26:41, 27:3-5
Heb. 3:13, 4:14-16, 11:24-26, 12:16-17, 13:5-6
1 Jo. 2:1
Rom. 6:23, 8:26-39
John 10:27-29
Rev. 17:14
Jas. 1:14-16

SIN
John 1:29, 8:34, 44
Psa. 90:8
1 Pet. 1:18-19, 2:24
2 Pet. 2:14
1 Jo. 1:7-10, 17, 3:4, 8-9, 5:17-18
Eph. 1:7, 2:1
Acts 8:22
Isa. 30:1
Gen. 3:6
Col. 3:5
Jas. 1:14-15, 4:17
Luke 11:4
1 Cor. 15:56

Gal. 5:19-21
Mat. 15:19, 25:41-46
Rev. 20:10, 15, 21:8, 27
Pro. 10:19, 14:34
Rom. 1:32, 5:12, 6:2, 16, 18, 21, 23, 8:13, 14:34, 12:9
Heb. 3:13, 9:26
1 Tim. 5:23-24
2 Tim. 2:19

SPEECH
1 Tim. 3:11, 4:12, 5:13
Tit. 2:8,3:2
Acts 26:26
1 Thes. 4:18, 5:14
Phi. 2:14
Ecc. 3:7
Mat. 12:36-37, 15:18, 26:73
Rom. 16:18
1 Pet. 3:10, 15
Eph. 4:25, 29, 5:4
Col. 3:8-9, 4:6
Jas. 1:19-20, 3:9, 4:11, 5:12
Pro. 6:17, 12:18, 22, 14:5, 15:1, 18, 16:14, 32, 17:4, 18:21, 20:20, 21:23, 29:5, 22

STRIFE
Pro. 1:19,10:12, 19, 13:10,14:29, 15:18,16:14, 28, 17:9, 27, 18:6, 20:3, 22:24, 23:29-30, 26:20, 28:28, 30:33
Jas. 4:1, 3:14-16
1 Tim. 6:4
2 Tim. 2:23
Gal. 5:19-21
Tit. 3:9
Phi. 2:1-8, 14
1 Cor. 13:4

THANKFULNESS
Rev. 4:9-11, 5:9-14, 7:11-12, 11:16-17

Acts 28:15
Luke 6:35
Rom. 1:8, 21, 6:17, 8:32, 14:6-7
Col. 1:3-5, 2:7, 3:17, 4:2
Heb. 13:15
1 Tim. 1:12, 2:1, 4:4-5
Eph. 1:16, 5:20
Dan. 6:10
1 Thes. 1:2, 2:13, 3:9, 5:18
Phi. 4:6
1 Cor. 1:4, 15:57
2 Cor. 2:14, 8:16, 9:15

TRUTH
John 1:14, 17, 3:21, 4:24, 8:32, 45, 14:6, 17:17, 19, 18:37
1 Sam. 12:24
1 Ki. 2:4
2 Ki. 20:3
1 Cor. 13:6
2 Cor.4:2
1 Tim. 6:5
2 Tim. 2:15, 3:7-8, 4:4
Rom. 1:18, 25, 2:2,8
1 Jo. 1:8, 3:18, 5:5-10
2 Jo. 4:3
3 Jo. 4,8
Eph. 5:15, 21, 25, 6:14
2 Thes. 2:10
Tit. 1:1, 14
1 Pet. 1:21-22
2 Pet. 1:12, 2:2
Jas. 1:18
Jer. 7:28
Pro. 3:3
Phi. 4:8
Psa. 51:6

UNITY
Phi. 3:16
Heb. 12:1
1 Cor. 1:10
Eph. 4:4-6
2 Cor. 10:5
1 Pet. 3:18

WISDOM
Rom. 11:33, 16:19
Isa. 5:21, 40:28
Col. 1:9, 29, 4:5
Psa. 44:21, 139:1-6
Jer. 10:7
1 Cor. 1:17, 21, 2:6-7, 13, 3:20
Eph. 1:17, 3:10-11
1 Chr. 28:9
Luke 16:15
Deu. 2:7
Mat. 6:8, 10:29-30
Dan. 2:21
Pro. 1:7, 3:14-15, 9:10, 29:15
Jas. 1:5, 3:5, 13

SOURCES

BROGAN, K., MD. 2016. A Mind of Your Own. Harper Wave Publishing, New York, NY. p19

CHAPTER 1
1. ZANNO, S. 2004. Dmitri Mendeleyev and the Periodic Table (Uncharted, Unexplored, and Unexplained). Library binding; Mitchel Lane Publishers, Inc. Pgs. 48
2. Female (FE-Iron) + (Male=Man) = Ironman. Pinterest, 2017. Retrieved November 14, 2017 from https://www.pinterest.com /jleonec/female-feiron-%2B-maleman-iron-man/
3. NICOLE, B. 2017. Goodreads: Quotes by Brigitte Nicole. Retrieved November 14, 2017, from ttps://www.goodreads.com/author /quotes/6441182.Brigitte_Nicole

CHAPTER 3
1. Phantasm: listed definitions 1-4. *Dictionary.com. Online Dictionary*. Oakland, CA: subsidiary of Search & Media, Inc. Web. 15 December, 2017

CHAPTER 10
1. Stress: *Dictionary.com. Online Dictionary*. Oakland, CA: subsidiary of Search & Media, Inc.
2. HOLMES & RAHE. SRRS: Elsevier Science; Journal of Psychosomatic Research, Vol.11, Iss.2, 1967, pp.213-18.
3. MECKLER, M. 2018. Patheos: Politics Red. Retrieved April 5, 2018, from http://www.patheos.com/blogs/markmeckler /2018/02/27-deadliest-mass-shooters-26-one-thing-common

CHAPTER 29
1. TOMATZKY, W; MICZEK, KA. Psychopharmacology (Berl). 1995. Alcohol, anxiolytics and social stress in rats. Sept; 121(1):135-44.
2. SCOTT, K.D.; SCHAFER, J.; AND GREENFIELD, T.K. The Role of Alcohol in Physical Assault Perpetration and Victimization. Journal of Studies on Alcohol 60:528–536, 1999.

CHAPTER 30
1. MCLAUGHLIN, M. Happy Wives Club Bolg. Retrieved January 22, 2018, from http://www.happywivesclub.com/staging/author/admin/page/41/

CHAPTER 31
1. SCHEVE, T. 2016. *How Stuff Works: How Bones Work.* Bone Marrow; Musculoskeletal System. Retrieved November 28, 2017, from https://health.howstuffworks.com/human-body/systems/musculoskeletal/bone2.htm
2. HUTT, M.S.R.; SMITH, P.; CLARK, A.E.; PINNIGER, J.L. 1952. *The Value of Rib Biopsy in the Study of Marrow Disorders.* St. Thomas Hospital and Medical School, London. (J. Clin. Path. 5), p.246
3. NATIONAL SCOLIOSIS FOUNDATION: Rib Thoracoplasty. Medical Updates & Resources, 2015. Rib Hump Q&A. Retrieved March 29, 2018, from http://www.scoliosis.org/resources/medicalupdates/ribthoracoplasty.php
4. THE FATHERLESS GENERATION. 2018. Statistics, pp.1-5. Retrieved February 2, 2018, from https://thefatherlessgeneration.wordpress. com/statistics/
5. Lee, M. Quote. Retrieved February 10, 2018, from https://www. oldquotes.com/author.php?tag=martha+lee
6. Boyd K. Packer quote, https://www.goodreads.com/quotes/34959-our-whole-social-order-could-self-destruct-over-the-obsession-with

CHAPTER 32
1. BLEDSOE, J. 2018. *The 7 Rings of Marriage:*blog post. Retrieved April 5, 2018, from http://jackiebledsoe.com/50-words-that-describe-your-dream-marriage/
2. Brides Magazine, August 11, 2015. *5 Wives Define What a Happy Marriage Means to Them.* Galleries: Topics, Married Life.
3. Dr. Chris Grace, PhD, July 20, 2015. Biola University Center for Marriage & Relationships; Blogs. Friendship, Marriage, Spiritual Intimacy; Posts. http://cmr.biola.edu/blog/2015/jul/20/5-qualities-happy-marriage/

CHAPTER 33
1. BEERY, J. 1890. Jesse Beery's Practical System of Colt Training: *From Old Catalog.* Parmenter Printing Co., Lima, Ohio. 207 pages.

CHAPTER 35
1. CHAPMAN, R.W. 1952. The Letters of Samuel Johnson, with Mrs. Thrale's Genuine Letters to Him, Vol. 1: 1719-1774; Letters 1-369. Oxford University Press, Cary, NC. ISBN: 978-0198185369
2. WALLER, J.F. 2014. Boswell and Johnson: Their Companions and Contemporaries. *Bloomsbury Academic Collections: English Literary Criticism, 18th and 19th Centuries*, p.103. Bloomsbury Academic Publishers, New York, NY. ISBN: 978-1472514509

She is…

Joyous, full of bliss

Outstanding, excelling beyond others

Nutty, full of wackiness

Enchanting, most alluring

Tantalizing, thrilling the senses

Trustworthy, your word is good as gold

Athletic, bounding with energy

Sensational, ever exciting

Happy, a bundle of joy

Alluring, so attractive

Noteworthy, having remarkable achievements

Kind, you have a good heart

She is Jonetta Shank, the love of my life and my entire world.

—Michael Shank